Biffi / Castrillón / Cordes / Cordeiro / Glemp
Groër / Honoré / López Trujillo / Maggiolini
Tomko / Willebrands

JOHN PAUL II

A PANORAMA OF HIS TEACHINGS

New City Press

Published in the United States by New City Press
206 Skillman Avenue, Brooklyn, New York, 11211
©1989 New City Press, New York

Translated from the original Italian
Giovanni Paolo II, Linee di un Magistero
©1988 Città Nuova, Rome, Italy

Cover design by Nick Cianfarani
Cover photo by G. Giuliani

745 81222

Library of Congress Cataloging-in-Publication Data:

Giovanni Paolo II--linee di un magistero. English.
    John Paul II--a panorama of his teachings / G. Biffi . . . [et al.].
      p.   cm.
    Translation of: Giovanni Paolo II--linee di un magistero.
    ISBN 0-911782-72-9 : $10.90
    1. Catholic Church--Doctrines--Papal documents.   2. John Paul II,
Pope, 1920-   I. Biffi, Giacomo.   II. Title.
BX1751.2.G483   1989
262.9'1 — dc20

                                                                89-39085

Printed in the United States of America

TABLE OF CONTENTS

PREFACE

There are many ways to mark a significant occasion like the tenth anniversary of the pontificate of Pope John Paul II. Because of his outstanding intellectual contribution to the Church and the world during the past decade, this book of essays on his thought is a very appropriate tribute.

The Holy Father brings several special qualities to his ministry in the See of Peter. As the only Polish pope in the Church's history, he brings a distinctive perspective to his role as "the visible source and foundation of the unity" of the Church (*Lumen Gentium*, 23). In its history as a Christian nation, Poland has often been a link between the Churches of the West and those of the East. Ecumenical dialogue with our Orthodox brothers and sisters has been one of Pope John Paul's priorities. Moreover, he has a deep appreciation of their unique cultural and religious heritage.

As his writings clearly demonstrate, the Holy Father is also a philosopher. He often uses a "circular" method, approaching a topic from several angles and examining its relationship with other ideas as he develops concentric circles around a core idea. He frequently returns to a key philosophical concept in addressing such diverse pastoral concerns as the Church's ministry to families and the public policies of nations. He speaks of "the truth about man," the truth about the human person "that will set you free." It is the human being's relationship with God which reveals full, authentic personhood and is the foundation of all ethical behavior. This anthropological concept also provides the basis of Pope John Paul's systematic approach to issues of social justice and world peace.

In his many pastoral visits, the Holy Father has given eloquent witness to his belief in the Lord Jesus and his commitment to the values of the gospel. He has seen firsthand both the richness and the poverty of various cultures. He has also become personally familiar with the needs of his brothers and sisters in a great variety of settings. Peter, indeed, is truly pastor of the whole world.

The essays in this volume reveal the breadth and depth of the Holy Father's teaching. They demonstrate the scope of his theological interest and the extent of his pastoral outreach, without, however, providing a systematic review of his comprehensive approach to social justice.

Each of the chapters in this book is based on the Holy Father's own writings: his encyclicals and other formal documents, his general weekly audiences in Rome, and his other published addresses, many of which were delivered on his pastoral visits throughout the world. The contributors frequently help the reader encounter the thinking of Pope John Paul in his own words.

In the initial essay on "Christ the Redeemer," Archbishop Jean Honoré, the Archbishop of Tours in France, examines this Christological theme which is at the very heart of the Holy Father's teaching. It was the topic of his first encyclical which provided a solid foundation for his subsequent catechesis. The mystery of redemption sheds light on the human condition, putting its true identity and full dignity in proper perspective.

The next article, by Hans Cardinal Groër, O.S.B., the Archbishop of Vienna and President of the Austrian Bishops' Conference, studies a key ecclesiological concept in Pope John Paul's teaching: As "the universal sacrament of salvation," the Church is both a "sign of salvation" and a "sign of unity" for the entire human family. No one is excluded from its embrace. The Church manifests the mystery of God's hidden plan of salvation in proclaiming the gospel and actualizing it in human lives.

Relying particularly on the encyclical, *Dominum et Vivificantem*, Giacomo Cardinal Biffi, the Archbishop of Bologna, offers a synthesis of the Holy Father's teaching about the role of the Holy Spirit in the Church. He explores the Spirit's role in the work of redemption and the enlightenment of the human family in regard to "the truth" about "man," about redemption, about evil, about the new life in Christ.

With this background — papal teaching about Christ the Redeemer, the Church, and the Holy Spirit in the Church — the reader is prepared to reflect on some of the Holy Father's pastoral priorities which flow from this teaching.

Jan Cardinal Willebrands, the President of the Pontifical Council for the Promotion of the Unity of Christians, reviews the search for full unity among Christians and Pope John Paul's teaching about, and commitment to, ecumenism. The Petrine ministry serves the unity of the Church in fidelity to the truth and in charity. However, it is very difficult to carry out this responsibility amid the complexities of contemporary Christianity. While ecumenical endeavors since the Second Vatican Council have been marked by both lights and shadows, it is essential that Christians continue to work together toward full unity so that the gospel may be proclaimed effectively everywhere. That is why Pope John Paul has frequently reaffirmed that ecumenism is a pastoral priority of the Church and has personally engaged in significant ecumenical activities — always attentive to the demands of both truth and charity.

The truth about Christ, "man," and the Church also has significant implications that extend well beyond the perimeters of the Christian churches. It impacts *all* cultures and peoples. Joseph Cardinal Cordeiro, the Archbishop of Karachi and President of the Pakistan Episcopal Conference, explores Pope John Paul's emphasis on the "religious sense of man" at a time when many members of the human family show little sensitivity for the spiritual dimension of human existence. By highlighting the innate human search for God, the Pontiff builds bridges to other religious traditions and cultures — for example, to Muslims in Morocco, Hindus in India, Buddhists in Japan, and Bushmen in Australia. He also frequently raises the concept of the "religious sense of man" when he meets with educators, scientists, and artists, as he seeks to counter the prevailing forces of secularization, materialism, and atheism.

A closely related topic is the Church's missionary activity and dialogue with the world. Josef Cardinal Tomko, Prefect of the Holy See's Congregation for the Evangelization of Peoples, summarizes the Holy Father's teaching on this subject under three rubrics: *what* the Church's mission is, *who* carries it out, and *how*. To be missionary, the Church must be evangelical; to be evangelical, the Church must be missionary. All members of the Church are co-responsible for its mission in the world in accord with their respective vocation and mission. Dialogue with other religions and cultures is the basic method of evangelization.

While the Holy Father's pastoral concerns and outreach are truly global, he also pays close attention to the basic unit of society: the family. Bishop Dario Castrillón, Bishop of Pereira in Colombia and President of the Latin American Episcopal

9

Council (CELAM), surveys Pope John Paul's pastoral concerns on the family. Again, the point of departure in his reflections on the family is the "truth" about "man" and Christ. He also frequently returns to three key factors which pertain to the very essence of the family: life, love, and community. As the "domestic Church," the family has a significant mission in the world and in the Church.

In his contribution to this volume, Alfonso Cardinal López Trujillo, the Archbishop of Medellín and President of the Episcopal Conference of Colombia, returns to the basic theme of "the truth of the human being in Christ." In particular, he reports how the Holy Father has used the theme in addressing various groups in Latin America—lepers in Marituba, poor farm workers in Recife, *campesinos* in Cuilapan, workers in Sao Paulo and Monterrey, lay leaders in Medellín, and youth in Belo Horizonte. The Cardinal then explores the meaning of the preferential love of the poor and authentic liberation in the thought of Pope John Paul II.

Jozef Cardinal Glemp, the Archbishop of Gniezno and Warsaw and President of the Polish Episcopal Conference, studies another key concept in Pope John Paul's social teaching: human work. The theology of work begins with the very first chapter of Genesis, in which God entrusts the earth to human care. Rather than being a curse, work enables us to share in the task of Christ's redemption. Building upon the great social encyclicals of the past, and reflecting upon his own experience, the Holy Father has happily further advanced the teaching of the Church's magisterium on this important topic.

The Church's mission of evangelization, as I have intimated, brings faith into dialogue with culture. Bishop Alessandro Maggiolini, the Bishop of Como in Italy, examines the nature and role of this dialogue in the teaching of Pope John Paul, especially as it relates to the development of a Christian society.

Of all the Holy Father's important pastoral concerns, one stands out in all its vibrancy and enthusiasm: his dedicated ministry to young people. Bishop Paul Cordes, the Vice President of the Pontifical Council for the Laity, brings this volume of essays to a lively conclusion by examining the significance of Pope John Paul's unprecedented Apostolic Letter to the Young People of the World. He knows their spiritual hunger and their need for a mentor in facing life's difficulties and approaching faith in a new way. He has taken on this role with great love, generosity, zeal, and, of course, personal competence.

I commend the editors of the New City Press and the authors of these essays on the publication of a significant book which serves to bring some of the most important themes of Pope John Paul's pontificate into a helpful synthesis. Any serious student of the Holy Father's teaching will find in these pages a wealth of material for further reflection and study.

Joseph Cardinal Bernardin
Archbishop of Chicago

CHRIST THE REDEEMER,
CORE OF JOHN PAUL II'S TEACHING

Archbishop J. Honoré

At the outset of his pontificate, John Paul II published an encyclical whose first words — *Redemptor hominis* — have a symbolic import. In their very conciseness, they express the core thinking of the Church's new shepherd. Indeed, it would not be rash to think that John Paul II, in this first encyclical of his magisterium, revealed the essence of his doctrine and brought to light what would be the very basis of his teaching. Didn't he acknowledge in the first pages of the encyclical that "Our spirit is set in one direction, the only direction for our intellect, will and heart — towards Christ our Redeemer, towards Christ, the Redeemer of man" (*Redemptor Hominis*, 7)? And he concluded with the assertion: "The Church stays within the sphere of the mystery of the Redemption, which has become the fundamental principle of her life and mission" (*ibid*.).

Thus did John Paul II, from the very dawn of his pontificate, bear witness to his belief in the core significance of the mystery of Redemption in the divine economy of faith and Christian salvation. He gave us, as it were, the key enabling us to understand and interpret the message that is repeatedly expressed in his encyclicals and numerous apostolic exhortations.

The purpose of this essay is to study the essential features of this message which is wholly rooted in the mystery of Christ the Redeemer. This is done, first, by clarifying the Christological thought of John Paul II in the pontifical texts themselves, and then by showing how his entire catechesis revolves around this main focus: the mystery of Redemption.

I. JOHN PAUL II'S CHRISTOLOGY

John Paul II's Christology is closely linked to a vision of the Christian mystery that is primarily defined by its *economical* aspect, that is, an approach to the realities of faith viewing them less in their truth *per se* than in their significance, less in their *ab aeterno* essence than in their relation to the order of salvation. Such a theological orientation comes mostly from the oriental tradition of the Greek Fathers: Saint Irenaeus and the Cappadocians. John Paul II's affinity with that tradition is striking. Following Saint Irenaeus' example, he is less intent on seeking — as a later analysis of the pontifical texts will show — to give an explanation of the dogmas than on *putting them in perspective*, that is, on showing the internal logic of a Revelation that orders them one to the other, defines how they are related, and brings to light their significance with regard to salvation, the ultimate reality of the human person's and the world's destiny.

A dynamic approach to the Creed

Therein lies the radically *dynamic* nature of John Paul II's teaching. He never separates the mystery of God from the human condition, the absolute of Revelation from the contingency of our existence, the truth of the Creed from its significance for the Christian faith. Such an approach, though inspired by the Irenaean or Cappadocian tradition, is also one that Vatican II has emphasized in several of its documents, particularly in the *Gaudium et Spes* constitution. There is no doubt that John Paul II, in his Christological teaching, is developing the Council's message expressed in many texts (especially *Gaudium et Spes*, 22), by stressing again and again the significance for the human person of the Incarnation of the Son of God "[that] fully reveals man to himself" (*ibid.*). And indeed it appears that this economical dimension of the revealed mystery is what highlights the Christology of John Paul II.

A global vision of faith

There is another aspect to this Christology, closely linked to the previous one: its *global nature*. The Redeemer of the human person, as John Paul II calls him to mind, is the Son of God who became a human being among human beings so as to insure their salvation. The mystery of the Incarnation is never separated from that of Redemption. They are one and the same mystery. This is also the economic view of Redemption.

13

Here, one must acknowledge the personal genius of John Paul II who seems to be perfectly attuned to the great contemplatives, especially the two masters he chose as patrons when taking his pontifical name: John, witness to the Incarnate Word in his gospel, and Paul, the apostle of the "mystery" in the epistles he wrote from prison. He does, of course, for homiletic purposes, comment on the events in the life of Christ: the narratives of the infancy gospel, for instance, in the encyclical *Redemptoris Mater*, or a specific parable such as that of the prodigal son in *Dives in Misericordia*, or yet again in the parenesis of his Wednesday exhortations to the pilgrims. Though when we re-read these texts, we are left with the impression that the core of his thought around which the whole of his teaching revolves, is the mystery of Christ. A telling example can be found in a homily on peace given in Saint Peter's Basilica on January 1, 1979. The sermon starts with a Christological evocation:

> By being born a man from the Virgin Mary in Bethlehem, God the Word accepts time. He enters history. He subjects himself to the law of human ebb and flow. He puts an end to the past. . . . He opens the future, the new Covenant of grace and of reconciliation with God. This is the new "beginning" of the new times. (World Day of Peace, January 1, 1979)

Indeed, John Paul II, trained at an early age in the disciplines of philosophy, goes straight off to the source and principle of knowledge. His intellectual process is to be understood above all as that of an intuitive thought which, facing a truth, is less concerned with its terms than with the need to penetrate its meaning. What matters is to grasp a significance before using a rational judgement; to understand the why before expressing the how of things. Isn't such a thought process the root of what has been called "a circular discourse" — so evident in the encyclicals — which causes thinking on a topic to unfold as a spiral, to work through successive developments, to go back and forth through the same necessary axis of reference which remains the focus of reflection? This very type of discourse is present throughout the first part of *Redemptor Hominis*, the encyclical *Dominum et Vivificantem*, and in *Redemptoris Mater*. The axis of reference around which the discourse is proceeding in these three major encyclicals of the pontificate, is the mystery of Christ the Redeemer, the "key truth of faith" (*Redemptor Hominis*, 1).

The analogy of faith

The upshot of this argumentation is that Christian dogma draws *its strong cohesion* from it. In a paradoxical way, the very totality of the redeeming mystery is, for the believer, the basis of its own credibility. For John Paul II—not one to put the transcendence of Revelation under a bushel—the redeeming event brought about by Christ is projecting on all the articles of the Creed a light lending to them the unity and coherence needed to gain the believer's adhesion. There isn't a single truth of faith, not a single provision of ritual, not a single demand of Christian praxis, that are not consonant with the testimonial of the fact that Jesus Christ, Son of God, became incarnate, died, and rose again. The entire "providential plan of the Most Holy Trinity" (*Redemptoris Mater*, 3) is understood and clarified thanks to this truth which is the foundation of faith and the source of all knowledge. This is the *crede ut intelligas* of John Paul II. Believing in Christ the Redeemer opens one's way to the understanding of the entire divine economy of salvation; it also draws from it the guarantee and assurance of a firm belief. And this is precisely the meaning of the following moving plea uttered on Christmas day 1978.

> I am addressing all the communities in their diversity. . . . Accept the mystery in which every human person has been living since Christ was born! Respect this mystery! Allow this mystery to act upon every human person! Allow it to unfold in the external conditions of one's earthly being. In this mystery is the strength of humanity. The strength that radiates on all that is human. Do not make this radiation difficult. Do not destroy it. For all that is human grows through this strength; without it, all perishes; without it all is ruined. (*Urbi et Orbi*, December 25, 1978)

As we will see later, John Paul II, with an astonishing sagacity, appropriates in his apostolic magisterium the thought process that really belongs to both a doctor of the faith and a theologian, and that had been identified by Vatican I with the *analogy of faith*. There is a correlation of dogmas between the two. One sheds light on the other. They understand each other in a reciprocity of significance. However, one must retain a hierarchy of value and meaning between the truths of faith, such as is already present in Revelation. Of this intelligence of the Creed, John Paul II is an exemplary master. Not only because he knows how to understand the relations and the harmonies uniting the revealed truths one to the other, but also and above all, because he is able to see them in the unique perspective that sheds light upon them, that is, the mystery of Christ the Redeemer. We will now see how he understands and develops this mystery.

II. THE DIVINE DIMENSION OF THE CHRISTOLOGICAL MYSTERY

As was shown above, the mystery of Redemption is the focal point of the reflection and teaching of John Paul II. It is the core of that thought which—in one glance, as it were—unites God and the human person, heaven and earth, the world and its Creator, the finitude of sin and the gratuity of salvation. The testimony of Jesus Christ is the keystone enabling us to grasp as a whole the Revelation of salvation *in its origin and principle*, the triune God, and the Revelation of salvation *in its accomplishment and end*, the reconciliation of the human person and his or her fulfillment in the glory of God. John Paul II makes a distinction between what he calls the "divine dimension" of the mystery and its "human dimension." This distinction, which underlies many speeches and exhortations, is explicitly highlighted in *Redemptor Hominis*.

One conviction is asserted with great distinctiveness: it is the Revelation of the Redeemer that enables one to meet and attain *the absolute of God's mystery*. Here, John Paul II remains very carefully in the footsteps of St. John the Evangelist. "No one has ever seen God. It is God the only Son, ever at the Father's side, who has revealed him" (*Dives in Misericordia*, 2, quoting Jn 1:18). This is expressed by an extremely concise formula in the encyclical *Dominum et Vivificantem*: "The gift of the Son expresses the most profound essence of God who, as Love, is the inexhaustible source of the giving of gifts" (#23). The absolute of the divine mystery is identified with love. Love is part of God's mystery. It is in the Son's Revelation that this love is manifested. And it is the Cross which tells and reveals the Father's love, as it reveals the very meaning of the creative act. "The Cross on Calvary through which Jesus Christ. . . 'leaves' this world, is also a fresh manifestation of the eternal fatherhood of God" (*Redemptor Hominis*, 9). In Jesus Christ "the Redeemer of the world. . . has been revealed in a new and more wonderful way the fundamental truth concerning creation" (*ibid.*, 8).

The Revelation of the Father

This love of God revealed by the redeeming event appears in the great encyclicals under various guises, as it were. But they all unveil something pertaining to the absolute. The gratuitous and thoughtful love of God who wants to reestablish the covenant of grace with enslaved people and a creation threatened to "futility" is the theme of *Redemptor Hominis*. The faithful love that perdures throughout history and follows "the providential plan for salvation" is a theme to be found in *Redemptoris Mater*. The merciful love that is always available for forgiveness and reconciliation is the entire message of *Dives in Misericordia*. The love identified with an active presence in the heart of people to turn them into children of God is the one depicted in *Dominum et Vivificantem*.

Starting from the redeeming act, John Paul II goes back to the source and principle, that is, God's mystery which is nothing but the mystery of an infinite love. The following text of the encyclical on mercy is typical of this thought process:

> This "making known" [of the Son] reveals God in the most profound mystery of His being. . . . "His invisible nature" becomes. . . *visible in Christ and through Christ.* . . . In Christ and through Christ, God also becomes especially visible in His mercy, that is to say, there is emphasized that attribute of the divinity which the Old Testament. . . already defined as "mercy." (*Dives in Misericordia*, 2)

The Revelation of the Holy Spirit

The encyclical *Dominum et Vivificantem*, devoted to "the Holy Spirit in the life of the Church and of the world," is also an illustration of this process of the pontifical thought which, leaning on the central pillar of Redemption, unfolds as if they were plants on a wall, the various doctrinal themes pertaining to the Holy Spirit.

This reflection is based on the words of Christ quoted in the Gospel of John, when he announces both his "departure" and the coming of the Spirit: "If I go, I will send him to you" (Jn 16:7). John Paul II, commenting on the text, posits as a principle: "There is no sending of the Holy Spirit. . . without the Cross and the Resurrection" (*Dominum et Vivificantem*, 24), and he goes on to say: "There is established a close link between the sending of the Son and the sending of the Holy Spirit."

It is necessary to notice from the outset all the importance and significance that the pope, master of the faith, attaches to this coming of the Holy Spirit linked to the redeeming event. In his eyes, it is "a new beginning" (*ibid.*, 14) that John Paul II deems to be a parallel of the beginning of the world, or first manifestation of the Spirit. The Spirit is gift, in the most absolute sense of the term. He is the most perfect expression of the Father's generosity. His coming ushers in the new covenant. Everything starts all over again with him.

Thought probes deeper into the comprehension of the mystery. Not only is the coming of the Spirit the major fruit of Redemption, but Redemption itself cannot be fully understood except through this coming of the Spirit. In the last analysis, and this might be the full message of the encyclical, the Holy Spirit himself reveals the redeeming event in its plenitude of significance and its power of salvation.

Indeed, John Paul II thinks that the Holy Spirit, present to Jesus in the Passion as he is during the entire life of Christ, gives to the death on the Cross its *sacrificial dimension*. The pope quotes from the Epistle to the Hebrews: "the blood of Christ, who through the eternal spirit offered himself unblemished to God. . ." (Heb 9:13-14), and he comments: "The Son of God, Jesus Christ, as man, in the ardent prayer of his Passion, enabled the Holy Spirit who had already penetrated the inmost depth of his humanity, *to transform that humanity into a perfect sacrifice* through the act of his death, as a victim of love on the Cross" (*Dominum et Vivificantem*, 40). This action of the Spirit is identified analogically by John Paul II with "the fire from heaven" that consumed the offering. "Fire of Love uniting the Father with the Son in the trinitarian communion" (*ibid.*, 41), he consumes the sacrifice and consecrates it in its perfection and full-ness. Thus is the pope able to affirm that "the redeeming sacrifice of the incarnate Word" is inseparable from this presence and this action of the Spirit in the oblation offered by Christ on the Cross (cf. *ibid.*, 40).

The Bishop of Rome's attention is drawn to another aspect of Redemption. One of the missions of the Spirit, announced by Christ himself (cf. Jn 16:8) is *to convince the world that it is sinful*. However, this denunciation of sin, which is the judgement of the world, is achieved by the Holy Spirit through the manifes-tation of sin's "relationship with the Cross of Christ" (*Dominum et Vivificantem*, 32). This doesn't only concern humanity's col-lective guilt since the beginning; this does, in John Paul II's thought, concern every personal sin "whatever the place or time it has been committed" (*ibid.*, 29). The Holy Spirit is present to the conscience so as to uncover the full evil of sin and "to point out its roots" (*ibid.*, 43). "In convincing the world concerning sin the Spirit of truth comes into contact with the voice of human consciences" (*ibid.*, 44). But he manifests and uncovers sin only by revealing the cost of a Redemption that decenters people from their evil atavism and frees them from fate. With a vigorous logic lending an undeniable originality to these pages of his encyclical, John Paul II strongly highlights this mission of the Holy Spirit who, at the heart of the world and of the human condition, exposes the presence of sin. The mystery of Redemption cannot truly be known unless one sizes up the real extent of sin's negating reality. Don't we have to understand that sinning against the Spirit means refusing to recognize ourselves as sinners and there-fore refusing to admit our need to be redeemed? (cf. *ibid.*, 46).

The mystery of Redemption is thus truly at the core of this reflection. One cannot talk about the mission of the Holy Spirit without putting it in perspective. The "departure" of Christ for death and Easter is the origin of this mission. But the Spirit is already present in the redeeming event since it is in him that Christ offers his death, and it is in "the power of the spirit" that he rises again. The Christological mystery includes and reveals the mystery of the Holy Spirit. Then comes the time of the Church. It is a time of mission among the people because it is first of all the time of the Spirit who, as John Paul II puts it, "gives life unceasingly by drawing on the riches of Redemption" (*ibid.*, 13).

In these pages of the encyclical evoking the transcendence of the trinitarian love, we encounter again the thought process described earlier, which is akin to that of the Greek Fathers. Starting from the divine *economy*, that is, from the completion of the salvific acts, and through some sort of induction derived from the analogy of faith, the believing thought of the pope meets mystery in its sovereign fullness: the fullness of love uniting the three divine persons. The latter are always seen in the perspective of the salvation achieved by Christ the Redeemer. The work of salvation, through the joint action of the Father, the Son, and the Spirit, reveals the depth of the divine mystery that sustains their trinitarian distinction and the infinity of their being and eternity.

Do John Paul II's vigorous teaching, his power of meditative suggestion enabling him to cross, by dint of prayer, the threshold of the thrice holy God, come from this thought process, found in all his writings, that permits him to discern the sovereignty of God and the infinite love revealed in all the initiatives of salvation whose center is Christ the Redeemer? Here is God's "philanthropy" — to use a word dear to the Greek Fathers' hearts — the most direct and richest path leading to the core of the unfathomable divine mystery.

III. THE HUMAN DIMENSION
OF THE REDEEMING MYSTERY

The mystery of Christ the Redeemer is also shedding light on the human condition. As the pope puts it "if we may use the expression, this is the human dimension" (*Redemptor Hominis*, 10). One could, with perfect exactness, talk about the mystery's anthropological dimension. What John Paul II offers in his first encyclical is a genuine reflection, an authentic philosophy of existence. *Redemptor Hominis* derives its full significance from a discourse whose very core is the human person, his or her nature and destiny. It is both a plea and a manifesto. This might be the text in which the teaching of the new pontiff appears at its most striking and incisive. Not that this is entirely new. Previous popes, especially Paul VI, had as we know turned their attention to human and social problems. However, in the importance he gives to the thematic of the human person, in the cohesion of his words that are anchored in faith, and also in the inner vibration of his style, John Paul II undeniably reveals in his first encyclical one of the axes of his deepest thought, giving the tone to his pontificate, as it were.

This unfolding of thought that we already perceived is to be found also in the evocation of the human condition enlightened by the redeeming mystery. The "circular discourse," starting from the central core, tends to broaden until it reaches newer and newer dimensions. This brings to mind not only a spiral motion but also the ebb and flow of tidal waves endlessly buffeting the seashore.

Christ reveals the human person to him or herself

The principle of such a reflection is contained in this sober encyclical statement: ". . .the mystery of the Redemption, in which the question of man is inscribed with a special vigor of truth and love" (*Redemptor Hominis*, 18). In the eyes of John Paul II, master and interpreter of faith, Christ and Christ alone expresses the human person in the truth of his or her existence and destiny. We remain an insoluble enigma to ourselves if we don't understand ourselves in Christ. Going back to the beautiful and long declaration of *Gaudium et Spes*, John Paul II comments on this major text of the conciliar constitution: "Christ. . . fully reveals man to himself" (*Gaudium et Spes*, 22), and writes: "Through the Incarnation God gave human life the dimension that he intended man to have from the first beginning; he has granted that dimension definitively" (*Redemptor Hominis*, 1). We find, here again, the very same idea that is developed about creation. And the latter also meets its "fundamental truth" in the "Redeemer of the world"; he is the one who frees it from "futility" (*ibid.*, 8).

This theme of Christ, revealer of the human person, is present as it were in all the pages of the encyclical. We can only bring to mind some of the most significant texts: "Christ the Redeemer fully reveals man to himself" (*ibid.*, 10). "Jesus Christ is the way to each man" (*ibid.*, 13). "In the mystery of the Redemption, man becomes 'newly expressed' and, in a way, is newly created" (*ibid.*, 10). John Paul II is so attached to this conviction that he bears witness to it in many exhortations and homilies. We will only quote from the homily devoted to Eternal Wisdom during his first visit to France: "Christ came into the world in the name of man's covenant with eternal wisdom. . . the covenant with eternal wisdom goes on within him. . . . In this covenant, man must grow and develop as man" (John Paul II, *France que fais-tu de ton bapteme?* — France, what of your baptism? [Paris: Centurion 1980], 140).

Not only does Christ reveal us in the truth of our being; he also reveals our vocation to us and gives us the very meaning of our existence. The human person's destiny is fully inscribed in the evangelical mystery of the God-Man. "Jesus Christ is the stable principle and fixed center of the mission that God himself has entrusted to man" (*Redemptor Hominis*, 11). In the famous speech he gave at UNESCO on June 2, 1980, John Paul II, with a certain apostolic pride, is claiming his right to evoke the destiny of the human person. Here is the very same assurance, *leitmotif* of an unchanging and indefectible conviction: "I am thinking about the fundamental link of the gospel, that is, of the message of Christ and of the Church, with man in his very humanity. . . . One must affirm man as such, and not for any other motive or reason: only such as he is. . . all the affirmations about man belong to the very substance of Christ's message and of the Church's mission" (*France que fais-tu de ton bapteme?*, 213).

More about the human person

In this thought as in his words, John Paul II never talks about human beings in abstract or purely conceptual terms. He talks less about humanity in general than about human persons, seen in the singularity of their beings and their destiny. *Redemptor Hominis* is rich in notations meant to convey that the topic is the individual human being, grasped at the heart of what makes him or herself, in his or her conscious and differentiated personality.

The very title of the encyclical is meaningful. Wasn't it on purpose that John Paul II called it the Redeemer of "man" and not of "men"? He wants to meet universality by starting with the concrete individual. It is the human person, identified in his or her unique reality who is the paradigm of human nature as seen in its totality. By looking at this human person, the pope meets all human persons. On this point, the pope seems again to have inherited the great tradition of the Greek Fathers, especially the Cappadocians who, in their anthropology, always gave priority to the concept of person over that of nature. Let's listen to John Paul II: "We are not dealing with the 'abstract' man, but the real 'concrete,' 'historical' man. We are dealing with each man. . . man in his unique unrepeatable human reality, which keeps intact the image and likeness of God himself" (*Redemptor Hominis*, 13). Further on, he stresses again: "Each man in all the unrepeatable reality of what he is and what he does, of his intellect and will, of his conscience and heart. Man, who in his reality has, because he is a 'person,' a history of his life that is his own and, most important, a history of his soul that is his own" (*ibid.*, 14).

The message of Christmas 1978, already quoted above, is imbued with the same fervor for the destiny of the human person, every human person; it bears the unmistakable stamp of *Redemptor Hominis* that John Paul II was then writing.

> In the name of this absolutely unique worth of each man, and in the name of this strength that the Son of God offers to each man by making himself man, I address this message first of all to man, to each man; wherever he works, creates, suffers, struggles, sins, loves, hates, and doubts; wherever he lives and dies; I address him today with the full truth of God's birth, with his message. (*Urbi et Orbi*, December 25, 1978)

The foundation of this anthropology that is so resolutely concrete is the fact that the Son of God, by becoming a human person, "united himself to each human person." John Paul II makes another reference to the conciliar constitution, quoting an essential passage (text of *Gaudium et Spes*, 22 in *Redemptor Hominis*, 8). As if he were afraid of not being heard, he repeats again: "We are dealing with 'each' man, for each one is included in the mystery of the Redemption and with each one Christ has united himself forever through this mystery" (*ibid.*, 13). Christ himself was that unique man who "worked with human hands, thought with a human mind, acted with a human will, and with a human heart he loved" (*Gaudium et Spes*, 22).

Clearly, this text has cast a spell on the pope who, in his encyclical, simply repeats the commentary of *Gaudium et Spes*, written when he was just Cardinal Wojtyla. Wasn't the whole purpose of the conciliar project to find an answer to the question: what is the human person?

> The answer cannot be separated from the problem of our vocation: we declare who we are by accepting this vocation and by achieving it. Through the intermediary of Jesus Christ, through the mystery of Redemption, we receive unceasingly the intense current of this calling faith through which we must find ourselves, must realize that we have been placed at the center of the Father's eternal plan. (Carol Wojtyla, *Aux sources du renouveau* — Sources of renewal [Paris: Centurion 1972], 63)

Being limited by the scope of this article, we cannot explain how this thought manages at the same time to straighten any anthropocentrical drift with which some people have wanted to identify the Council's work, and to denounce the positivism inherited from social sciences leading to the conclusion that "man is dead." Suffice it to simply point out to the close correlation established by the pope, after the Council, between the revelation of the Christological mystery and the knowledge of the "mystery of man," to use the words of Vatican II.

The human person, way of the Church

As we know, the Church is always present to John Paul II's eyes and meditation. No matter how keen his reflection on matters of faith is, how lofty his teaching seems to be, he never forgets the mission entrusted to the Church. This is evident as early as this first encyclical in which every page evokes and confirms this mission of the Church. An illustrative word, that of "route" or "way" is used in the entire development and lends to it a kind of incantatory strength.

If "Jesus Christ is the chief way for the church," and if he is also "the way to each man" (*Redemptor Hominis*, 13), the fact remains that, in order to fulfill her mission, the Church must follow an apostolic project. The latter is *serving human persons*, human persons understood in the integrity of their being and their vocation as children of God. In fact, a person who meets the Church is wide of the mark. We experience at the same time our inner divisions and our fragility in the face of the world's threats. The contemporary human person doesn't escape this condition: more than ever, the currents of history lead us to ask yet more fundamental questions while we are exposed to drifts that are more and more alienating. And we are precisely the human persons whom the Church must find and meet. "This man is the primary route that the Church must travel in fulfilling her mission" (*ibid.*, 14). "He is the way for the Church — a way, that in a sense, is the basis of all the other ways that the Church must walk" (*ibid.*).

We will not follow John Paul II on all the paths that he draws for the Church in order to meet this genuine challenge of serving human persons, which he greets with a spontaneous cry: "Again and always man" (*ibid.*, 16). Suffice it to note that the mission of the Church, within the logic we described earlier, is to want herself "strongly united with each man" (*ibid.*, 18). No one is excluded. Every one of us must be able, when encountering the Redeemer of the human person to "enter to him with all of his own self, he must appropriate and assimilate the whole of reality of the Incarnation and Redemption in order to find himself" (*ibid.*, 10). In this mission, "the Church also recognizes the way for her daily life, which is each person" (*ibid.*, 22).

The new advent

In John Paul II's view, this apostolic mission of the Church is urgent and concrete because of the redeeming event's imminent third millenary. Has anyone noticed the fact that the new pontificate entered from the outset in the perspective of an impending day for which Christians should be prepared? In its very exordium, the first encyclical evokes the horizon of the year 2,000. And it concludes with a remainder of this "new Advent of humanity" which ought to renew and stimulate the Christians' attention to this mission at the service of human persons through the spread and witnessing of the gospel.

An identical call of apostolic urgency is set forth in the encyclicals devoted to Divine Mercy, to the Holy Spirit, and to the Mother of the Redeemer. Such an insistence might surprise some people. But they would know little about the spirit of John Paul II. Like John XXIII, he watches "the signs of the time" and the mutations of history. He knows that his pontificate is unfolding in an era marked by the accelerated evolution of progress' techniques, of the planetary relationships between peoples, and by the changes in mores that they bring forth. In his eyes, the question of the human person, of his or her vocation and future, appears to be a decisive one. In the next millenary, humanity will cross a new threshold. This millenary is that of the Christian era; it will be celebrated by the "Great Jubilee." And in our time of preludes, John Paul II wishes to be the "watchman" recalling the Christians to the way they must open so that human persons — whether today or tomorrow — may meet Jesus Christ the Redeemer. In this New Advent, the pope is conscious of being the "forerunner" whose teaching and action have one sole aim: affirming the Church in her mission which is to make Jesus Christ possible for every person and for all people.

Archbishop Jean Honoré
Archbishop of Tours (France)

(Translated from the French by Nelly Marans)

THE CHURCH
SACRAMENT OF SALVATION

Hans Cardinal Groër, O.S.B.

The very first message of Pope John Paul II, in the celebration in the Sistine Chapel of October 17, 1978, already indicates his great interest in the theology of "Church." He reveals his program: "The area we want to give special attention to is the ecclesiological" (*Urbi et Orbi*, October 17, 1978). With this statement of intention he also gives the viewpoint from which he will view the Church. He quotes Pope John XXIII, whose words in a slightly different form became the basic theme of *Lumen Gentium*: "The Church is the universal sacrament of salvation" (#1).

A BROADER CONCEPT OF SACRAMENT

In borrowing this terminology, he already shows that "sacrament" cannot be understood in the narrow limits in which it has been used in the theology of the seven sacraments. He shows this same viewpoint in other statements about the Church, e.g., the Church "is the sacrament of community" (discourse to the Secretariat of the Bishops of Latin America and Panama, March 2, 1983), she is the "universal sacrament of salvation" (*Instrumentum Laboris*, 2), she is sent forth "to proclaim reconciliation and to be a sacrament of reconciliation in the world" (*Reconciliatio et Paenitentia*), and, it is important "to serve the Church, the universal sacrament of salvation" (to young people, Lima, February 2, 1985).

Pope John Paul II himself emphasizes in one of his statements that he uses "the concept 'sacrament' in a wider sense than the traditional one which meant the signs instituted by Christ and administered by the Church." We have here "a wider and perhaps also a more ancient and fundamental meaning of the word 'sacrament.' " Our first step is to understand to what extent his wider use of the term sacrament coincides with the general usage and to what extent it differs, in his statements above and in many others like them.

POINTS OF CONTINUITY IN TERMINOLOGY

There is general theological agreement about sign and instrumental causality. "Sacrament" refers to that which both signifies and causes something — something which is different from the sacramental sign itself. Pope John Paul II makes this clear when he says: "A sacrament in the generally accepted sense of the term is in fact a 'visible sign.' In this sign or through this sign God gives us himself, his transcendental reality, and his love. The sacrament is a sign of grace, an effective sign. It not only signifies something, by expressing it in a visible way in the manner of a sign, it also produces it, enabling us to receive the grace so that the work of Redemption which God foreordained from eternity and fully revealed in Jesus Christ is actualized and accomplished in us" (general audience, June 28, 1982).

This talk of sign and efficiency with regard to sacrament already introduces new elements when this theological concept is employed in the "wider" sense mentioned above and is applied to the Church. This is not only likely but undeniable when he undertakes to develop central ideas of *Lumen Gentium,* v.g.: "The Church is a kind of sacrament of Christ, that is, a sign and instrument of deepest union with God as well as for the unity of all humankind" (#1). The Church as sacrament, he says, not only signifies and brings about union with God in the realm of grace, but also signifies and brings about unity among all humankind in the natural realm. This striking new aspect of "sacrament" apparently leads the pope to add at once: "The text does not say 'the Church is a sacrament' but rather 'like a sacrament,' which is to say that we must speak of the sacramentality of the Church as analogous, but not identical, to the seven sacraments instituted by Christ and administered by the Church" (general audience, September 8, 1982).

This point deserves our full attention, since we have here a significant and far-reaching expansion of our understanding of the Church. She is "sign of salvation" *and* "sign of unity for the human race." Since this unity is already based upon and guaranteed by our common human nature, his idea here seems to refer to a unity for the whole human race brought about by grace, in a way that earlier theology did not so readily perceive. A statement at the close of 1979 points in this direction: "We must give thanks for the grace of God given to each and every human being, not just to those of us here, but to every brother and sister in every corner of the world" (homily, December 31, 1979). "Each and every human being"—does this involve formal adherence to the Church? He continues: "Our thanksgiving is like a grand synthesis. The whole Church is part of it since she is . . . a sacrament for all" (*ibid.*).

This has a very universal tone: "for *all* persons," without exception. It seems to include both Church as sacrament of salvation *and* Church as sacrament of unity for the human race. The apparent universality of the sacramental mission and activity of the Church which is but mentioned here becomes quite explicit when Pope John Paul II says at the outset of his pontificate: "We have to take up the dogmatic constitution *Lumen Gentium* once more to study with renewed energy the nature and mission of the Church, the nature of its existence and activity. We must do this not just to bring about a living communion in Christ of those who believe and hope in him but also for a greater and stronger unity among the whole human family. For the Church is the universal sacrament of salvation and of the unity of the human race" (*Urbi et Orbi*, October 17, 1978).

POINTS OF DIFFERENCE IN TERMINOLOGY

Before trying to throw light on the theological background of this sacramental universalism, we must mention the most significant ways in which it differs from the narrower understanding of "sacrament" in traditional theology.

First of all, this concept is used for much that has not hitherto been considered and dealt with precisely as "sacrament" in the technical theological sense. The fact that sacrament functions as a sign leads us to consider the visibility of creation, especially of the body as sacramental: "Sacrament or sacramentality—in the broadest sense of the word—is related to the body and presumes a theology of the body. 'Body' implies that which is visible, it refers to the visibility of the world and of humanity" (general audience, July 28, 1982). From this perspective we can begin to see a "basis for the sacramental character of the whole Christian life" (general audience, September 8, 1982). This is a reference to the "sacrament of creation" and we hear that "the original order of grace proceeds from the sacrament of creation" (*ibid.*). Analogously we hear of a "sacrament of redemption" (*ibid.*) described as that "profound mystery," "the mystery of Christ and the Church, which gives the Church its sacramental aspect" (*ibid.*). So we see two distinct orders with their respective differences, yet each having a sacramental character:* "The new sacramental economy, founded on the sacrament of redemption, is a gift of Christ to his bride the Church, and is distinct from the original economy of salvation. For it comes to us not on the basis of original justice and innocence, but rather in view of our sinfulness and our heritage of original sin (the state of fallen nature)" (*ibid.*).

A significant difference becomes apparent when we examine the concept of sacrament more deeply, a difference that distinguishes it considerably from mystery. From a purely philological point of view, spiritual and theological tradition has translated the Greek *mysterion* by the Latin *sacramentum*. *Mysterion* seems to imply an understanding of sacrament as that which hides and reveals; and this suggests meanings and interpretations that do not correspond to what is meant here by "the wider or widest sense" of sacrament. Pope John Paul II spoke of this most explicitly: "'Sacrament' is not synonymous with 'mystery' " (general audience, September 8, 1982). The reference notes to this rather surprising statement remind us that this concept has a long history extending over centuries and that the meanings of the term can be quite relative, as when we read: "the historical meaning of the word 'sacrament' must begin with the Greek word *mysterion* which, to tell the truth, refers in the book of Judith to the battle plans of the king" (*ibid.*).

---

* *The context states clearly enough that here we should not think either of the "sacraments" of the Old Testament (like circumcision) on the one hand, or of the "sacraments" of the New Testament on the other. We are dealing with the sacramental order of creation on the one hand, as well as with the sacramental order of salvation on the other.*

SACRAMENT AND MYSTERY

We can explore more fully the difference which Pope John Paul II's statements indicate between sacrament (of salvation, which is the Church, and sacrament in general) and the concept of mystery. A first point of difference lies in the fact that mystery suggests the hiddenness and inaccessibility of the divinity, while sacrament suggests revelation and disclosure. "The mystery remains hidden — in God himself — so that even after its proclamation or revelation it never stops being mystery and being proclaimed as mystery. Sacrament consists in the presentation of this mystery in sign" (*ibid.*).

A second point leads us to see mystery as a profound spiritual reality which lies typically and essentially outside our vision and comprehension as human beings. Since its essence is concealed from us and yet deemed necessary for our well-being, it is of great significance that it be communicated to us by something comprehensible for us who are essentially creatures of matter and sight, that it become visible in the sacrament. We "can assume" (certainly "in the wider context of scripture which reveals God's saving plan 'in the beginning' "), that the word *mysterion* means "the mystery," first hidden in the mind of God and then revealed in human history. This is indeed a "great" mystery in view of its importance: This mystery, as God's plan of salvation for all humanity, is in some way the central theme and content of all Revelation. It is what God as creator and father desires above all else to convey to us in his word. This enables us to appreciate the context for sacrament: "The sacrament presupposes the revelation of the mystery and it presumes also its faith-filled acceptance on our part. At the same time it is more than just the proclamation of the mystery and its acceptance in faith. The sacrament consists in the presentation of this mystery in a sign which serves not only to make the mystery known but also to bring it to realization in us" (*ibid.*).

We have already touched on the third point of difference. Mystery, in the framework of this terminology, is understood as idea, intention, concept; sacrament is understood as the carrying out of the divine mind and will. The pope teaches this clearly when he says: "The sacrament is a visible and efficacious sign of grace. Through the sacrament the mystery hidden in God from eternity is brought to realization . . . the mystery of our call to holiness in Christ through God and the mystery of his determination to accept us as his child. This is *accomplished* in a mysterious way under the veil of a sign which makes visible the mystery that lies beyond our nature and becomes *operative* in us under its sign" (*ibid.*). (*Emphasis ours*)

SACRAMENTAL THEOLOGY OF POPE JOHN PAUL II

On the basis of this clarification, we can now attempt a brief presentation of the sacramental theology of Pope John Paul II, in which we find the precise development of his teaching on the Church as the universal sacrament of salvation.

As we have briefly tried to summarize so far, that which originates in God and is in its nature entirely ordered to becoming a sign, receives a sacramental character in order to point to him so we can become aware of his existence and action. This applies fundamentally to creation, especially in view of its material aspect and appearance, since these guarantee its visibility which is precisely what we are dealing with here. Without this corporeal dimension, it could not fulfill its sacramental role. "Thus corporeality, in some general way at least, enters into the very definition of a sacrament, which is a 'visible sign of an invisible reality,' that is, of a spiritual, transcendent, divine reality" (general audience, July 28, 1982).

In this sense the "mystery of creation" must be understood fundamentally "as a 'making visible of the invisible' " (*ibid.*, September 29, 1982). Its sacramentality is evident in the state of original grace: "The holiness originally bestowed on the human person by the creator is part of the reality of the 'sacrament of creation' " (*ibid.*, October 6, 1982).

With regard to human beings this "sacramental" process comes especially to the fore and this is in view of our corporeality. "The Christian vision of the human person attributes a unique function to the body because it helps reveal the meaning of human life and purpose. Corporeality is a particular way of being and acting proper to the human person. This fact is first of all anthropological in nature: the body discloses the person, 'it is an expression of the person,' and is therefore God's first word to humanity, a kind of 'primordial sacrament or sign in the midst of a visible world communicating the invisible mystery hidden

32

in God from all eternity' " (Congress for Catholic Education, November 1, 1983).

The so-called sacramentality of creation and of the body enables us to understand marriage in an analogous way. "It is on the basis of the sacrament of creation that we must understand the sacramentality of marriage in the beginning (the primordial sacrament)" (general audience, October 20, 1982). Holy scripture throws light on this connection in many ways. "The author of Ephesians speaks of the body . . . in its metaphorical . . . as well as in its concrete meaning, that is, the human body in its perennial masculinity and femininity, in its perennial destiny to union in matrimony" (*ibid.*, July 28, 1982). The letter to the Ephesians "speaks in fact of marriage as a 'great' sacrament in a broad exhortatory context, that is, in the framework of moral appeals that the life of a Christian . . . shows forth the principles by which he lives" (*ibid.*, October 20, 1982). "Christ himself in his dialogue with the Pharisees (Mt 19:3-9) confirms, first of all, the existence of matrimony. If we reflect on this enough, we will see that matrimony is in some measure the primordial sacrament, the prototype of all the sacraments of the New Covenant" (*ibid.*).

The "fact that Christ takes his stand on the level of that primordial sacrament" allows us to understand "that he speaks out of the depths of the mystery of Redemption, the Redemption of the body." Here we find "key statements on the theology of the body," for "Christ makes his pronouncement as it were out of the divine depths of the 'Redemption of the body' (Rom 8:23). This pronouncement is of fundamental importance for the person, created bodily, male and female" (*ibid.*, October 27, 1982). Here we have the bridge from the sacrament of creation to the sacrament of redemption. "For Redemption means a 'new creation'— it embraces all creation" (*ibid.*).

THE SACRAMENTALITY OF THE CHURCH
FACT, MANNER, DEVELOPMENT

Efforts to give a comprehensive explanation of the "classical text" of Ephesians 5:21-33 (cf. general audience, August 4, 1982 and October 27, 1982), has already made it clear "that the Church herself, on the basis of Christ's relationship to her is the 'great sacrament,' is the new sign of the covenant and of grace, rooted in the depths of the sacrament of redemption, just as matrimony has arisen from the depths of the primordial sacrament as the original sign of the covenant and of grace" (*ibid.*). But we need to consider: "The sacramentality of matrimony is not only the model of the sacrament of the Church (and Christ), it constitutes an essential part of our new heritage: the sacrament of redemption which has been bestowed on the Church of Christ" (*ibid.*, October 20, 1982).

"Human conjugal love remains forever a great sacramental expression of the fact that 'Christ loved the Church and gave himself up for her' (Eph 5:25)" (to fourteen American bishops, *ad limina* visit, September 24, 1983). This parallel must not be misunderstood as remote or arbitrary. For the relationship between Christ and the Church "is both a revelation of the mystery of salvation and its realization in history, a revelation and realization of the mystery of God's loving election, 'hidden' in him from eternity. In this revelation and realization, the mystery of salvation embraces the special movement of love between Christ and the Church, and thus expresses itself in a very suitable way, in view of its similarity to the relationship between husband and wife in matrimony" (general audience, August 18, 1982).

From this analogy we become aware of the depths of the relationship between Christ and the Church and this in turn sheds light on the sacramentality of the Church. "The Church is in fact the body which — being subject to Christ the head in all things — receives everything from him who makes her his body. She receives the fullness of salvation as a gift from him who 'gave himself up for her' even to the very end. This 'self-giving' of Christ even to death on the cross out of obedience to the father receives here a decidedly ecclesiological meaning: Christ 'loved the Church and gave himself up for her' (Eph 5:25). By a total self-giving out of love he formed the Church as his body and builds her up constantly as her head. As head he is the savior of his body and, likewise, as savior he is the head. As head and savior of the Church he is also the spouse of his bride" (general audience, August 18, 1982)

The body has, as we know, a revelatory function; it is a sign of the invisible, which it makes visible. The body is essentially "sacramental." Since the Church is the *body* of Christ, we must see her therefore as a sacrament of Christ. Thus we read: "The only way to the father is Christ. He is made visibly present and active through the ministry of the visible Church, his sacrament"

(Bishops' Synod, 1983). And likewise in another place: "The Church lives and grows as the body of Christ and therefore all human suffering completes the sufferings of Christ by virtue of the Church's union with him in love. Human suffering completes his suffering just as the Church completes the redemptive work of Christ" (*Salvifici Doloris*, 24).

This already indicates a particular direction in which the sacramentality of the Church operates. Indeed, his repeated insistence on these facts directs our attention to the ways in which this sacramentality is operative in history. On this point the pope teaches: "The Church is already a sacrament simply through her existence as a community of reconciliation which witnesses and presents to the world the work of Christ. She is a sacrament furthermore through her office as guardian and interpreter of scripture, the good news of reconciliation. She makes the plan of God known from generation to generation and shows everyone the way to full reconciliation in Christ. Finally, she is sacrament through the seven sacraments which, each in its own way, 'build up the Church'" (*Reconciliatio and Paenitentia*, 11). Hence one can say, "that the Church's sacramental character is manifested by all seven sacraments through which she fulfills her mission of sanctification" (general audience, September 8, 1982).

Concerning the Church as sacrament of salvation and the way it operates in that capacity, Pope John Paul II speaks theologically in another context of how this originated: "As sacrament, the Church arises out of the paschal mystery of Christ's 'farewell,' living in his perennial 'coming' in the power of the Holy Spirit whom he sent as Paraclete, the Spirit of truth. Precisely this is the essential mystery of the Church" (*Dominum et Vivificantem*, 63). This thought is developed further: "It is in the mission of the Holy Spirit, invisibly present, that the son, who had 'departed' in the paschal mystery, 'comes back,' and is always present in the mystery of the Church, at times hiding himself, at times showing forth in her history which he continues to direct. All this happens in a sacramental way, through the working of the Holy Spirit who continues to create and give life out of the riches of Christ's Redemption. As the Church becomes ever more aware of this mystery, she sees herself more clearly above all as sacrament" (*ibid.*).

UNIVERSAL MISSION OF THE CHURCH
AND SALVATION

In this context we meet the already familiar statement: "the Church is 'the sacrament . . . of the unity of all humankind' " (*Dominum et Vivificantem*, 64). This statement is further developed: "Obviously it is a question of the unity which the human race with all its variety has 'from God and in God.' This unity is rooted in the mystery of creation and it receives the new dimension of universal salvation with the mystery of Redemption. Because God desires 'that all be saved and come to the knowledge of truth' (1 Tm 2:4), Redemption includes all humanity and in a certain way all of creation. The Holy Spirit is at work in this universal dimension of Redemption by virtue of Christ's 'farewell.' Therefore the Church, whose mystery is rooted in the Trinitarian plan of salvation, has every reason to regard herself as the 'sacrament of the unity of the entire human race' " (*Dominum et Vivificantem*, 64).

This universalism is expressed in a rather cautious formulation in an address in 1983, in which the pope says: "The kingdom of God is already present 'in a mysterious way' in history and is at work in those who accept the Lord. It is present in the reality of the Church, which is the sacrament of salvation and a mystery whose boundaries are known only to the father of mercy who desires the salvation of all." In looking at this universalism carefully we can distinguish a double aspect. The first is expressed thus: "The mission of the Church involves the *whole* person, his temporal and eternal salvation. It includes the totality of pastoral care, the entire religious, spiritual and material realm" (Einsiedeln, June 15, 1984). We can add this statement too: "Every walk of life is , as a 'Christian' vocation, rooted in the sacramentality of the Church" (to the youth of the world, March 31, 1985). In a second aspect "the Church specifically manifests itself as 'sacrament,' that is, as sign and instrument of unity, peace and reconciliation among *all* peoples, nations, social classes and cultures" (in St. Mary Major, December 8, 1985). (*Emphasis ours*)

Looking at both these aspects of universalism, by which the Church understands herself as sacrament of salvation for the individual as well as for everyone without exception, we are reminded of that passage in *Lumen Gentium* which, without mentioning the word salvation, speaks of the Church in her sacramentality as "sign and instrument of the deepest union with God *as well as* for the unity of all humankind." Such a way of speaking, in view of the way Pope John Paul II develops his teaching, suggests that both elements mentioned are derived from the fact of salvation.

Finally, we should like to recall a tension which remains and which the Church, as she reflects on herself in her pilgrimage, can never resolve. Although she is "body," visible and thereby a means of divine Revelation she always conceals something of her essence and must await the "revelation of the mystical body in its complete and perfect reality" (Angelus, August 21, 1983). Since the Mother of God is not only "the type and the perfect image of the Church" (*ibid.*), we can say with Pope John Paul II "that with Mary's assumption into heaven the parousia of the Church has already begun" (*ibid.*).

CONCLUSION

The limits of this article and the practical impossibility of consulting all the sources do not permit us to give an exhaustive presentation of all the perspectives which this topic opens up. Still it does show the spiritual initiative which the pope's sacramental vision wishes to give, and what he wishes to emphasize in his teaching on the Church. It reflects a central concern of his pontificate and the guiding features of his theology.

This insight might be helpful for better understanding and organizing many other statements and directives, which at first seem unrelated. There can be no doubt that the concept of the Church as the universal sacrament of salvation dominates the thinking of Pope John Paul II. We can expect that his words, therefore, as words of a teacher and guide, will always revolve around this truth, and that his actions will consistently bear it out.

Hans Cardinal Goër, O.S.B.
Archbishop of Vienna
(Austria)

(Translated from German by Eugene Selzer)

THE ACTION OF THE HOLY SPIRIT IN THE CHURCH AND IN THE WORLD

Giacomo Cardinal Biffi

The name of the Holy Spirit recurs very frequently on the lips of John Paul II, who sees in him the secret source of all ecclesial vitality, the guarantor of a possible transformation of the world, the principle of a renewed human psychology, the hope of a more complete intercommunion among the Churches.

The large number of quotable expressions from the most varied contexts would make it difficult to present the reader with a synthesized version of his teaching. Fortunately, in the encyclical *Dominum et Vivificantem* (May 18, 1986) the pope himself has given us an explanation, in quasi organic fashion, of this theme. Our text, then, will offer first a substantial basis for our inquiry, but this will be confirmed by and integrated into affirmations found in many other pontifical pronouncements.

The limited space available here obliges us to use a presentation of the material that might be called "rhapsodic," and even to employ a type of discourse so bare as almost to seem schematic; it will, however, be enhanced by our assiduous recourse to literal quotations.

I. WHO IS THE HOLY SPIRIT?

1. "Who is the Holy Spirit? He is God himself; he is the Third Person of the Most Holy Trinity. He was sent to each one of us by the Father and the Son. He is the supreme gift, and remains constantly in us."[1]

John Paul II does not care much for direct speculations about the Holy Spirit in himself, on his "properties," and his "appropriations," on his origin and his place within the life of the Trinity.

Of course, the pope is not ignorant of the most classical questions posed by the scholastics on all these points. As may have been noticed in the words just quoted, he speaks explicitly of the Holy Spirit's mission to us, as coming from the Father and the Son. This is something clearly taught by the word of God, and is not a matter of controversy among the Churches.

What is a matter of controversy is, instead, the question of whether this "mission" also presupposes a "procession" from the Father and the Son within the mystery of trinitarian life.

The Latin Church responds affirmatively, and the pope also reiterates this doctrine, while stressing at the same time the substantial identity of this formula with the Greek formula: "from the Father, by the Son."[2]

It is interesting to remark that when the Creed of Constantinople is cited (which in the original Greek text does not include the *filioque* found in the Western tradition) a clear ecumenical intent led to the omission of the entire phrase referring to the "procession." And in his letter to Patriarch Dimitrios dated June 4, 1980, we read that "this is one of the points which can and must be resolved in the dialogue between the two Churches."[3]

In his catechesis, John Paul II does not fail to remind us that the Third Person "proceeds *by way of the will* and *in the mode of love,*" and that this is the "commonly accepted doctrine in the teaching of the Church, and hence is something sure and binding."[4]

However, as is normal in instruction which never forgets that it must be "pastoral," the Holy Spirit is considered rather in his action *ad extra,* and in the fruitfulness which he displays throughout the universe.

II. THE HOLY SPIRIT AND THE CHURCH

2. The mystery of the outpouring on humanity of the Spirit of God — the mystery of Pentecost — follows from the mystery of the Redemption; and from the mysteries of the Redemption and of Pentecost there follows and there subsists the mystery of the Church.

It all flows from the risen crucified One, who, as is clear from John's account, gives the Spirit "as it were through the wounds of His crucifixion."[5]

Laying special emphasis on the action of the Paraclete in the work of Redemption, the pope throws light on the secret of the origin and of the subsistence of the new Christian phenomenon in the world. "The Redemption is totally carried out by the Son as the Anointed One who came and acted in the power of the Holy Spirit, offering Himself finally in sacrifice on the wood of the cross. And this Redemption is, at the same time, constantly being carried out in human hearts and minds — in the history of the world — by the Holy Spirit, who is the 'other Consoler.' "[6]

3. The starting point, then, is "the reality of the Resurrection, by which, in a relationship of causality rather than of chronology, Christ gave the Holy Spirit to the Church as a divine gift, and as the unfailing and inexhaustible source of sanctification."[7] Hence it can truly be said that "the Pentecostal event started on the day of the Resurrection."[8]

For this reason Christians can be described as "those who, accepting the mystery of Christ's Resurrection, submit their hearts to the power of the Holy Spirit, whose coming down upon them takes place constantly."[9]

4. At the moment in which the Holy Spirit is sent by the risen Christ, the "time of the Church" begins. "The time of the Church began at the moment when the promises and predictions that so explicitly referred to the Consoler, the Spirit of truth, began to be fulfilled, in complete power and clarity, in the Apostles, thus determining the birth of the Church."[10] Therefore, "in a certain way, the grace of Pentecost is perpetual in the Church."[11]

As is obvious, Pentecost is not something ephemeral; it is not an event which, once over and done with, is immediately thrust aside by history's forward march; it is a lasting happening by means of which God creates for himself a people which is his, and thus concerns himself with the salvation of the world. "The Holy Spirit comes in order to remain with the Church and in the Church, and through her, in the world."[12] "The Pentecost event does not belong only to the past; the Church is always in the Upper Room that she bears in her heart."[13]

5. This is the reason for the permanence, for the vitality, for the strength of the Church; this, and not her organization, nor the human talents of her members, nor the means she may have at her disposal, but the presence within her of this divine and personal energy. In virtue of the Holy Spirit "the Church lives, works, and grows to the close of the age."[14]

This is also the secret of her youth and of her constant renewal while all other institutions sooner or later grow old and decay.

The Third Person of the Trinity "is the source and dynamic power of the Church's renewal."[15] For this reason the "task of renewal of the Church. . . cannot come about if not in the Holy Spirit, that is, with the help of his light and his power."[16]

We come, then, to understand what the Church truly is in her deepest reality. "The Church is the sign and instrument of the presence and action of the life-giving Spirit."[17]

III. THE HOLY SPIRIT AND THE TRUTH

6. Special attention is given to the action of the Holy Spirit in the Church, with reference to the truth which enlightens and saves.

It is precisely the Spirit who makes the Church, in some manner, the everlasting "epiphany" of the invisible God, amidst the darkness of the world. "The supreme and complete self-revelation of God, accomplished in Christ. . . continues to be manifested in the Church through the mission of the invisible Consoler."[18]

The Church can neither forget nor misrepresent the truth of Christ precisely in virtue of this immanent Master of hers, who "preserves in the memory and in the teaching of the Church all that Christ has transmitted to humanity from the Father."[19] Here we have the correct insight permitting us to grasp the prerogative of the Church's infallibility. "The Holy Spirit, then, will insure that in the Church there will always continue the same truth which the Apostles heard from their Master."[20]

7. According to Jesus' words, then, the Spirit leads us to the entire truth, because, "if it is true that all the fragments of the truth should be welcomed with love and honored, wherever they may be found, it is also true that only the truth, whole and entire, really saves. And that truth, whole and entire, also includes what people naturally find difficult to accept, for instance the mystery of Christ's self-emptying through His Passion and death on the cross."[21]

8. This certain relationship with the truth given us by the Holy Spirit is what establishes and inspires our mission in the world. "The Pentecost event. . . is a truth-happening. Precisely because they are enlightened by the truth, possessed by it, and convinced

of it, the disciples of the Lord feel themselves capable of announcing it to the world with absolute certainty."[22]

9. The Holy Spirit — as the pope so opportunely remarks — will help the Church and all believers especially in discerning the authentic fruits of the Second Vatican Council "from everything which may instead come originally from the Prince of this world."[23] Such discernment is doubtless necessary and urgent in our day.

IV. THE HOLY SPIRIT AND EVIL

10. "Evil," wrote Leon Bloy, "has an angelic origin; because of this, human reason struggles to explain it." But the "Spirit of Truth knows the original reality of the sin caused in the will by the 'father of lies.' "[24] The Holy Spirit, being the Spirit of truth enlightens us also about the existence and about the dramatic character of the evil which besets the life of us human beings.

It is a light we need especially today, because in the Christianity of our times people refuse to take seriously the tremendous and real enigma which we are called upon to combat. Some persons may believe that by acting in this way they are adopting an attitude which they consider inspired by the gospel; but in fact it has no basis in the word of God.

John Paul II, instead, with his firm grasp on reality, has always been aware of evil, just as he is always aware of the Lord's victorious power; this is why he speaks of "Redemption" (*Redemptor Hominis*), of "mercy" (*Dives in Misericordia*), of the Spirit who throws full light upon and combats the "mystery of iniquity" (*Dominum et Vivificantem*).

11. A human being's radical disintegration starts in the conscience (which is in itself one of God's highest gifts) when it claims to set itself up as an interior tribunal liberated from any objective norm of behavior.

"To us, created in the image of God, the Holy Spirit gives the gift of conscience, so that in this conscience the image may faithfully reflect its model, which is both Wisdom and eternal Law, the source of the moral order in mankind and in the world. 'Disobedience,' as the original dimension of sin, means the rejection of this source, through a person's claim to become an independent and exclusive source for deciding about good and evil."[25]

Under the guidance of the Spirit we must get back to understanding that "the conscience, therefore, is not an independent and exclusive capacity to decide what is good and what is evil. Rather, there is profoundly implanted within it a principle of obedience vis-a-vis the objective norm."[26] "A result of an upright conscience is, first of all, to call good and evil by their right name"[27] and this is also a primary "fruit" of the Holy Spirit.

12. The Spirit helps us not to forget that there exists — and will always exist, until the end of the human experiment — an active and permanent power of evil which operates in the world — a truth which today is widely rejected among Christians. "The analysis of sin in its original dimension indicates that, through the influence of the 'father of lies' throughout the history of humanity there will be a constant pressure on us to reject God."[28]

There is, and there will always be, until the glorious coming of the Lord, an unending force of opposition to the Father's saving initiative. "The history of salvation shows that God's coming close and making Himself present to mankind and to the world, that marvelous 'condescension' of the Spirit, meets with resistance and opposition in our human reality."[29]

13. A cultural attitude which evidently flows from this opposing power is materialism, "both in its theoretical form, as a system of thought, and in its practical guise as a method of interpreting and evaluating facts, and likewise as a corresponding program of conduct."[30]

We need to remark, by the way, that "materialism, as a system of thought in all its forms, means the acceptance of death as the definitive end of human existence."[31] From this point of view, human life is exclusively a question of "existing in order to die."[32] Fortunately, the Spirit reacts, within us and in the world, against this dark impulse towards self-destruction and this lack of understanding of all true values.

From this source arise those "signs of death" which are becoming more and more frequent in the human race: abortion, euthanasia, the armament race, nuclear destruction, mass starvation, and so on. But we know that over this desolate landscape the Spirit of life is ever blowing, and we already possess the first fruits thereof.

14. He is also the Spirit of liberty, who reveals to us and preserves in us our nobility and the high destiny which is ours.

"When, under the influence of the Paraclete, people discover this divine dimension of their being and their life, either as persons or as communities, they can free themselves from the various kinds of determinism, which arise mainly from materialism's cast of thought, from its practice, and its corresponding methodology."[33]

Here we have the basis for our hopes: "in the struggle between good and evil mankind shows itself all the stronger thanks to the power of the Spirit, who acting within the human soul, makes our desires bring forth fruit in goodness."[34]

V. THE HOLY SPIRIT AND LIFE

15. In the pope's teaching the Third Divine Person is contemplated most particularly as the principle of life: *Dominum et Vivificantem*. He is "the One in whom the inscrutable Triune God communicates Himself to human beings, constituting in them the source of eternal life."[35]

John Paul II adopts an eminently unified and concrete vision of life. Certainly, he does not ignore the two levels, of creation and of grace, which can and must be cultivated distinctly in every redeemed creature. But he never forgets that everything in this order of Providence must be viewed in the unity of God's design, without juxtaposition of levels, or extrinsic exclusiveness. He does not hesitate to locate the Holy Spirit even at the source of what we might call "natural" existence.

In the Spirit, who, according to the Genesis account, "moved over the waters," we should see both the principle of the gift of existence, and also "the beginning of God's salvific self-communication to the things that He creates."[36] For this reason, "the Holy Spirit, consubstantial with the Father and the Son in His divinity, is Love and uncreated Gift, from whom there flow, as from their source, all God's bounties towards creatures: the gift of existence to all things through creation, the gift of grace to mankind through the entire economy of salvation."[37]

16. In fact, the Holy Spirit is, as the gospel story makes clear, the protagonist of the event of the Incarnation, and precisely "in the mystery of the Incarnation the action of the Holy Spirit

'who gives life' reaches its culminating point. It is not possible to give life, which in its fullest mode is in God, except by making it the life of a Man, like Christ in His humanity, endowed with personhood by the Word in the hypostatic union. And at the same time with the mystery of the Incarnation there opens up in a new way the source of this divine life in the history of mankind: the Holy Spirit."[38]

17. "Let us never grow weary of praising the Holy Spirit, the inexhaustible fount of our life in Christ."[39] As a consequence and an extension of the Incarnation we receive a new birth which determines in us the infusion of a new divine life. "But the birth, or re-birth, happens when God the Father 'sends the Spirit of His Son into our hearts. . .' Sanctifying grace is the principle and source of our new life — a divine, supernatural life."[40]

18. As a principle of life immanent in the soul the Holy Spirit can be defined as "the law of the redeemed person" since he, dwelling in the heart of the redeemed person "transforms the subjective character of the person, making it interiorly submissive to the law of God and to his salvific plan."[41]

In particular, he introduces into the person and into the world the great divine will of reconciliation. "He acts as an interior light which leads the sinner to acknowledge his sin. At the same time that he inspires repentance. . . . He arouses sentiments of trust in divine love which pardons, and in the efficacious action of the Savior. . . then, in Pentecost, he inaugurates the work of reconciliation of individuals among themselves."[42]

19. In this way we find, starting in the heart of the individual, a true transformation of the world by the action of the Spirit. "The Triune God who 'exists' in Himself as a transcendent reality of interpersonal gift, imparting Himself in the Holy Spirit as a gift to mankind, transforms the human world from within, from inside hearts and minds. Along this path the world, made to share in the divine gift, becomes ever more human."[43]

20. The sacraments themselves which express and give life, draw their efficacy from the energy of the Paraclete, so that, "the Church is the visible dispenser of the sacred signs, while the Holy Spirit acts in them as the invisible Dispenser of the life which they signify. Together with the Spirit, Christ Jesus is present and acting."[44]

21. And, while he "is active in the heart of sacramental and liturgical life, inspiring the new law, promoting missionary activity, creating and restoring unity, the Holy Spirit is also

mysteriously present in the non-Christian religions and cultures."[45]

22. The liturgy rightly calls Him *Consolator optime* because in fact it is he who, by means of all who are willing to become his instruments, can alleviate and give meaning and value to all the misfortune and suffering found in our human condition. "It is the Spirit of the Father alone who gives consistency to the little that we human beings can do to console and comfort our sick and afflicted fellows."[46]

23. Another characteristic element of this new life is a new capacity for prayer. "The breath of divine life, the Holy Spirit, in His simple and ordinary way, expresses Himself and makes Himself felt in prayer. . . . Wherever people are praying in the world there the Holy Spirit is found, for He is the living breath of prayer."[47]

"Our difficult age has special need of prayer. . . . In many individuals and many communities there is a growing awareness that, even with all the rapid progress of technological and scientific civilization. . . mankind is threatened, humanity is threatened. . . . And thus they are discovering prayer, in which the Spirit 'who helps us in our weakness' manifests Himself. In this way the times in which we live are bringing the Holy Spirit closer to the many who are returning to prayer."[48]

24. With this multiform action the Paraclete enlivens humanity. Here John Paul II recalling to mind a phrase of St. Irenaeus, which is usually quoted in a mutilated fashion, reaches this conclusion: "Thus, it can truly be said that 'the glory of God is the living person; yet our life is the vision of God.' A human being living the divine life, is the glory of God; and the Holy Spirit is the hidden Dispenser of this life and this glory."[49]

Giacomo Cardinal Biffi
Archbishop of Bologna (Italy)

(Translated from Italian by Richard Arnandez, FSC)

NOTES

1. To young people, Murrayfield (Great Britain), May 31, 1982
2. General audience, May 20, 1985
3. Letter to Patriarch Dimitrios, June 4, 1981
4. General Audience, November 20, 1985
5. *Dominum et Vivificantem*, 24
6. *Ibid.*
7. Homily at Pentecost, May 25, 1980
8. *Ibid.*, May 17, 1986
9. Homily at Christ the King parish, Rome, May 18, 1980
10. *Dominum et Vivificantem*, 25
11. *Ibid.*   12. *Ibid.*, 14
13. *Ibid.*, 66   14. *Ibid.*, 61
15. *Ibid.*, 2
16. Epistle *To The Council of Constantinople* I, March 25, 1981, 7
17. *Dominum et Vivificantem*, 64
18. *Ibid.*, 7
19. Homily at St. Monica parish, Ostia (Italy), May 8, 1983
20. *Dominum et Vivificantem*, 4
21. *Ibid.*, 6
22. During the Vespers in the Sanctuary of Divine Love, June 7, 1987
23. *Dominum et Vivificantem*, 26
24. *Ibid.*, 35   25. *Ibid.*, 36
26. *Ibid.*, 43   27. *Ibid.*
28. *Ibid.*, 38   29. *Ibid.*, 55
30. *Ibid.*, 56   31. *Ibid.*, 57
32. *Ibid.*   33. *Ibid.*, 60
34. General audience, December 17, 1980
35. *Dominum et Vivificantem*, 1
36. *Ibid.*, 12
37. *Ibid.*, 10
38. *Ibid.*, 52
39. Homily at Anchorage (Alaska), February 26, 1981
40. *Dominum et Vivificantem*, 52
41. General audience, August 3, 1983
42. *Ibid.*, May 25, 1983
43. *Dominum et Vivificantem*, 59
44. *Ibid.*, 63
45. At the Theological Congress of Pneumatology, March 26, 1982
46. Homily at a Mass for the sick, June 5, 1983
47. *Dominum et Vivificantem*, 65
48. *Ibid.*   49. *Ibid.*, 59.

JOHN PAUL II AND THE SEARCH
FOR FULL UNITY AMONG CHRISTIANS

Jan Cardinal Willebrands

"AN IRREVERSIBLE COMMITMENT" IN PATIENCE, TRUST, AND HOPE

It is challenging to undertake to trace a partial account of what John Paul II has taught on the subject of ecumenism in the ten years since he began his pontificate — a pontificate so promising for the Catholic Church's ecumenical commitment — and to do this within the necessarily restricted limits of a chapter in a book dedicated to his magisterium as a whole. This is true not so much because of the complexity of the material which, by its very nature, does not lend itself to ready exemplifications, but especially because of the abundance of the arguments, acts, addresses, visits, and journeys which, in these last ten years, have seen John Paul II become the protagonist, inspirer and con-tinuator of that movement stirred up by the Spirit,[1] which is generally called by the name of "ecumenism."

Leaving aside a philological explanation of the word, but stressing that the expression "ecumenical movement" as com-monly employed, implies many realities which are distinct from one another and sometimes diverse from one another,[2] it seems that we need to begin these reflections by recalling some words of the Holy Father which are so clear and emblematic that they cannot leave room for any doubt, and even less for rejecting every Christian's duty to personally work for unity. The follow-ing words reveal the intentions of John Paul II: "I shall never tire in the exercise of my Petrine ministry — which is a service of unity in truth and charity — insisting on this point and encourag-ing every effort performed in this direction, at every level where we meet with our other Christian brethren. Perhaps this common witness is often limited, because we have not reached complete agreement about its contents. But this realization should neither stop us nor, still less, discourage us. Even now, taking stock of all that is possible, and seeking at the same time to make progress towards a common profession of the apostolic faith, we today shall proclaim Christ and draw nearer to unity. . . . I wish to re-state that the Catholic Church is irreversibly committed to the ecumenical movement, and that she wishes to contribute thereto with all her power. For me, as Bishop of Rome, this constitutes one of my pastoral priorities. It is an obligation that I must fulfill in a special way, precisely in virtue of the pastoral responsibility which is peculiarly mine. This movement has been stirred up by the Spirit; and I consider myself profoundly responsible with regard to it. I humbly beg the Spirit for his light and strength, so that I may serve the holy cause of unity in the best possible way."[3]

The words we have just quoted come from an allocution addressed to the Roman Curia in the Basilica of St. Peter's on June 28, 1985, the vigil of the feast of Saints Peter and Paul, patrons of the Roman Church. The occasion itself lent a character of solemnity to the allocution, in which John Paul II commemorated the twenty-fifth anniversary of the founding of the Secretariat for the Unity of Christians.[4]

If it still remains difficult for me, as I mentioned above, to summarize the pope's ecumenical involvement, it seems to me that John Paul II succeeded very well in summing up in that allocution the lights and the inevitable shadows of the movement of Christians towards unity; and, something perhaps even more important, he succeeded in saying what was essential, next to which all the rest can be coordinated and harmonized, proposing to all a model to follow, the path which is practicable today, the path in which he personally has undertaken to walk most resolutely.

The presence at the Council of observers from the Orthodox Churches, from the ancient Oriental Churches, and from the main Churches and Christian communities, the creation of the Secretariat for Unity, the dialogues, meetings, gatherings, official visits, and all that has been going on during these last years, "in season and out of season" (2 Tm 4:2). . . none of this can be justified, in fact, apart from the determination, as John Paul II affirms, to show to the world our unity in proclaiming the mystery of Christ. For the divisions among Christians, in our civilization, as we move towards the year 2,000, the legacy of a sad but finished past, compromise the very credibility of the proclamation of the gospel to every creature.[5]

49

For this reason the pope underscores the fact that in his ministry as Bishop of Rome he has exhibited all possible solicitude in encouraging meetings with our other Christian brethren.

Someone might object that this common witness of Christians is often limited, or, worse still, useless; because they have not succeeded in reaching full agreement on the contents of their faith. But the pope advises all such not to abandon themselves to discouragement, to pessimism, and to distrust, which might slow down or nullify all the efforts made in this direction; because, if as of now, we do together all that it is possible to do, and seek to make progress towards a common profession of the faith, Christians can together proclaim Christ, and thus draw nearer to unity.

The prefix "re-" used by the Holy Father when he says: "I want to *re*-affirm. . ." aligns his words and his ecumenical commitment with the acts performed by his predecessors, John XXIII and Paul VI. This "pastoral priority" is one which the pope understands not as a prerogative of his own pontificate, but as the logical continuation of a process which arose in the Church, a legacy which he, from the beginning of his pontificate, from the allocution he pronounced to the conclave which elected him, willed to take up.

The concluding words in the sentence quoted from the allocution of June 28, 1985, also express another idea: "This movement has been stirred up by the Holy Spirit, and I consider myself profoundly responsible for it." The pope assumes, in the very first place and for the faithful of the entire Catholic Church, the grave responsibility of working for this movement dictated by the Spirit, whose light and strength he begs for (two terms, the first of which refers to the intellect, while the second refers to the heart, and both of which are able to expand to unbelievable dimensions the limited capacities of human possibilities), in view of serving this holy cause of unity in the best possible way.

In these years of his pontificate the pope has acted in ways that have written a new history of the relationship among Christians, and which, because of their examplarity, are the eloquent proof of how much the pope is doing to make clear his responsibility for striving for the growth of communion among Christians, and the reestablishment of full unity among them.

We should not, however, imagine that this is going to be an easy task, or that the search for unity can be limited to spectacular gestures, or well-publicized meetings. For this reason the encouragement that the pope has given to the ecumenical movement is, in a certain sense, all the more precious, and must be considered not only with regard to "our other Christian brethren," but also as applying to the Catholic Church itself, so that within it there may be an increase in awareness and in the desire of collaborating with other Christians—of living *with* them, not just alongside of them; understanding their mentality and their susceptibilities, without, for all that, surrendering our own positions, without generalizations or compromises, as easy as they are useless.

But there is another reason why the address of June 28, 1985 is such an important one. In it the pope also thanked God "for what he has accomplished through the Secretariat for the Unity of Christians during these twenty-five years; for what he has accomplished in the other Churches and ecclesiastical communities, and by means of them." In other words, he willed, in a programmatic discourse, addressed to his closest collaborators in the service of the Church, to take note of and approve all that is being done in the Catholic Church to make effective the teaching of the Council and to inspire research which not only enriches the field of theology, but spreads out in all directions, touching every aspect of Christian life.

However, the euphoria of the Council has long subsided. Anyone who re-reads today the words pronounced by Pastor Marc Boegner on February 18, 1965—some twenty-five years prior to the Holy Father's allocution which we have been quoting—on the occasion of the visit paid to the Ecumenical Council of Churches by Cardinal Augustine Bea, might perhaps find that he sounds a bit overenthusiastic to us today: "How many obstacles have already been overcome! When I think of the total ignorance of each other in which the Christian Churches lived from the time of their separation and for centuries thereafter: Orthodox, Catholics, Presbyterians, Anglicans, Lutherans and others; when I think of the incomprehension which characterized us, nay, of the great diffidence, the great hostility, and even of the many struggles, conflicts, and calumnies; when I think of all this, and now breathe the air of Rome, in a totally new climate which has been built up in these last few years, once more I exalt the action of the Holy Spirit and the miracle of God's grace."[6]

The fact is that neither diffidence, hostility, conflicts nor calumnies have entirely disappeared, nor that today the Churches everywhere perceive, and with the same intensity, the progress made. Still, without exaggerating, one can say that "obscurantism" is done with; that this is indeed "ancient history"; and by obscurantism I mean diffidence, hostility and calumnies beyond appeal. I mean the explicit will, on the part of Christians, to live their faith in declared and reciprocal antagonism.

Marc Boegner, on the other hand, was expressing a conviction of the moment, which left greater room for a hope of rapid solutions. The theological dialogues initiated after the Council between the Catholic Church and almost all the great Christian denominations[7] have shown that the way is a long one, strewn with real or supposed obstacles, often to be traversed only with difficulty. In other words, it has been easier to "separate" from one another than it now is to come back to full fellowship.

Still, it was necessary to try this new experience of fraternity among the Churches, this desire — still rather fragile for a while — to give up offensive polemics based on prejudices, and on that determination not to place in jeopardy again a "vain prestige," but rather to keep in mind the apostle's exhortation: "let not contentions, envyings, animosities, dissensions, detractions, insinuations, and manifestations of pride be among you" (2 Cor 12:24).[8] It was necessary to proceed with the new experience of fraternity among the Churches, with the rigor and in conformity with the impetus given by the Council, even as there faded away the remembrance of the first "sign" given by the Spirit to the conciliar event.

The Spirit works unceasingly in the history of the Church. From the very first day of his pontificate, John Paul II asked the delegates from the other Churches who had come in large numbers to attend the solemn inauguration of his ministry, to say to those whom they represented that "the Catholic Church's obligation towards the ecumenical movement, as was solemnly expressed in Vatican II, is irreversible."[9]

The Holy Father, a little short of one year from his election (and there were those who declared that his election was a "master stroke" by the Spirit), called together those responsible for the Secretariat for the Unity of Christians to tell them about his desire to go to Constantinople to visit his brother in the East, Dimitrios I. The project was quickly carried out.[10] On his return to Rome the pope spontaneously pronounced a phrase destined to become a most efficacious slogan, to define the relationships between Rome and the Orthodox, a phrase which he used again later on in various texts and official discourses: "The Church must learn once again to breathe with its two lungs, the Eastern one and the Western one."

Events multiplied. I do not think it right for me to describe certain ones while passing over many others which will have to be omitted from these notes, for lack of space. Nor does it seem to me opportune to apply to this choice a selective criterion. It is better, then, to outline in as explicit a manner as possible, the *teaching* that John Paul II has given while carrying out his ecumenical obligations. In the second part of this chapter we have examined this teaching, in his own words. From this examination there has resulted a true ecumenical summa: the correct view of unity, the definition of the ecumenical undertaking, which must be above all an encounter in truth and love, progressively brought about according to the inspiration of the Council, through conversion of hearts and in holiness of life; an individual and collective renewal ever sustained by prayer; an activity tending to show the unity among Christians which already exists, and to create occasions for giving common witness, even in favor of mankind and humanity; a catechesis which may remove prejudices and false interpretations; the duty of laboring for unity; and finally patience, trust and hope, which should accompany all action tending towards the reestablishment of full communion among Christians.

Such, then, is his teaching. His actions, moreover, have been and are in harmony with this teaching, a practical catechesis, a gift offered to all, not only to those who have patience, trust, and hope.

Everywhere, throughout the world, John Paul II has met with the faithful of other Churches and Christian communities[11] welcoming them with a fraternal condescension capable of removing at once not a few intolerant and equivocal attitudes. He has proposed to our faith the example of Sister Maria Gabriella, a young Trappistine nun who offered her life and her vocation for the cause of unity, and whom he proclaimed Blessed. (Nor should we forget Maria Gabriella's fervor, and her simple but essential passion for unity.) At Assisi on October 27, 1986, he welcomed a great many brethren from the other Churches to join in prayer for peace, giving with them an example of profound and humble trust in the power of prayer. He decided that an Orthodox Metropolitan should preach during the Vespers celebrated in the Basilica of St. Peter's.[12] With a warm embrace he greeted the Ecumenical Patriarch on December 6, 1987, in the Basilica of St.

Peter's; and that embrace will remain a symbol and a pledge of his determination to continue walking in the path towards full communion. John Paul II willed that Dimitrios I, on that same Sunday, should stand with him at the central loggia of the Basilica for the solemn recitation of the Angelus. As a pilgrim of reconciliation he visited the Lutheran parish in Rome. In Canterbury he prayed, kneeling side by side with the Archbishop Primate of the Anglican Church. "For this is the message which you have heard from the beginning, that we should love one another" (1 Jn 3:11).

WHY ECUMENISM IS A PASTORAL PRIORITY[13]

In the first place, unity is a great gift which must be defended and safeguarded. "The unity of the Church is a deep mystery which transcends our understanding, our efforts, our desires. . . . Christ, from the beginning, gave this unity to his Church; at the same time, it must always be sought and reconstructed by the whole body of Christians" (*Insegnamenti*, III/2 p. 1823). In fact, "the different conditions of life of the individual Christian Churches can never justify discord, disagreements and divisions in the profession of the one faith, and in the exercise of charity" (*Slavorum Apostoli*, 13).

The mysterious unity bestowed by Christ on his Church "transcends all human causes of division" (*Insegnamenti*, I, p. 1989). In fact, "one of the salient aspects of Christian truth that Vatican II once more placed into focus, is the profound, even if still imperfect communion which exists even now among all those who are justified by means of faith in Jesus Christ, who are incorporated into him by baptism and are animated by the Holy Spirit. And for this reason we rightly recognize them as our brethren in the Lord" (*ibid.*, III/1, p. 1994).

This, then, is the task we faced: "to restore, in the peace of reconciliation, the unity that was gravely damaged" (*Slavorum Apostoli*, 13). We need to seek "a vital unity in the real communion of various elements" (*ibid.*, 26). We must "build communion together" (*ibid.*). We need "to re-discover, through prayer and dialogue, the visible unity in perfect and total communion, the 'unity which is neither absorption nor fusion' (*ibid.*, 26). Unity is a meeting in truth and love granted to us by the

Spirit" (*ibid.*, 27). "All of us who are Christ's followers must, therefore, meet and unite around Him. This unity in the various fields of the life, tradition, structures, and discipline of the individual Christian Churches and ecclesial communities, cannot be brought about without effective work aimed at getting to know each other and removing whatever blocks the way to perfect unity" (*Redemptor Hominis*, 11). "We also need to banish far from our memories the disputes and condemnations of the past, leaving them to the mercy of God. We must strive to construct together a present and a future more in line with Christ's will for the unity of all his disciples" (*Insegnamenti*, VIII/1, p. 1997).

We have said that unity is an authentic encounter in *truth*. Consequently, "the union of Christians cannot be sought in any compromise between the various theological positions, but only in a common encounter in the most ample and mature fullness of Christian truth. This is our desire, and theirs also. It is a duty of mutual honesty. Vatican II affirmed that there is nothing more foreign from ecumenism than that false irenicism from which the purity of Catholic doctrine suffers, and in which its genuine and precise meaning is obscured" (*ibid.*, III/1, p. 1892).

And here is what follows: "Authentic ecumenical dialogue requires of the theologians a great maturity and certainty in the truth professed by the Church; it requires of them a particular fidelity to the teaching of the magisterium. Only by means of such a dialogue can 'ecumenism' that great heritage of the Council, become an ever more mature reality; in other words, only on the path of a great self-commitment of the Church, inspired by the certitude of faith and by confidence in the power of Christ in which, from the start, the pioneers of this undertaking were distinguished" (*ibid.*).

Another characteristic of the common search for all the truth in view of reaching unity, is that it should be carried on in love. "Love increases by means of the truth, and truth draws near to the person by the help of love" (*ibid.*, V/2, p. 1942) "Christian truth cannot be assimilated without charity. Only if we reestablish among ourselves and constantly enrich a real climate of fraternal charity, can we make progress in the truth. Indeed, in so far as we are guided by the Spirit of truth, who is the fount of all fraternal charity and who manifests himself in this fraternal charity, can we understand the truth revealed to us; only his light can guide us to the whole truth" (*ibid.*, VIII/1, p. 1994).

Here the pope amplifies and deepens his teaching, saying: "In this sense the Council, when indicating the path of ecumenism, spoke of conversion of heart, stressing that 'we should beg of the divine Spirit the grace of sincere abnegation, of humility and meekness in serving, of fraternal generosity of soul towards others' (*Unitatis Redintegratio*, 7). Reciprocal humility, inspired by love and by the worship of truth, must guide us in our constant search for the most appropriate ways of restoring once again unity among our brethren" (*ibid.*).

It is known that in the context of the words of the Conciliar Decree on Ecumenism which we have just cited, the Council affirmed that "the soul of the ecumenical movement consists in conversion of heart, holiness of life, along with private and public prayer for unity" (*ibid.,* 8). This is what the Council called "spiritual ecumenism." And these ideas too are amply expounded in the teaching of John Paul II.

In the first place: *holiness of life*. In his address at Canterbury during his pastoral visit to England, the pope affirmed with vigor: "Still, such hopes and programs will be of no use at all if our struggle for unity is not rooted in our union with God. In fact, Jesus told us, 'In that day you shall know that I am in my Father, and you in Me, and I in you. He that has my commandments and keeps them is the one who loves Me, and I shall love him, and will manifest myself to him' (Jn 14:20-21)" (*Insegnamenti,* V/2, p. 1941).

From this we perceive the relationship existing between "exterior unity" and such intimacy with Christ. "The external unity for which we pray will be the outgrowth, the flowering of that intimate union with Christ which all the faithful indistinctly should have: bishops, priests, consecrated souls, laity—with this sole difference that some can devote themselves more to bringing it about, some less. There cannot be any unity among the faithful if there is no deep union—of life, of thought, of the soul, of intention, of imitation—with Christ Jesus; nay, unless there is an intimate seeking for interior life in union with the Trinity itself, as Vatican II so well brought out, saying, 'The more closely the faithful are united with the Father, the Word, and the Holy Spirit, so much more intimate and easy will be the action by which they will increase their mutual brotherhood' (*Unitatis Redintegratio,* 7)" (*Insegnamenti,* IV/1, p. 145).

From the striving for sanctity on the part of individuals the pope goes on to the wider concept of an "*individual and col-*

lective renewal." "Through our conversion and this individual and collective renewal, we are already serving the cause of ecumenism (cf. *Unitatis Redintegratio*, 6-7). However, I should like to add that in its turn, our labor for unity favors such renewal; in fact, when we undertake a true dialogue with our brethren in common faithfulness to the gospel, we and they see ourselves mirrored in this dialogue, and are spurred on mutually to an ever greater fidelity. Thus, all of us can put into practice the words of St. Paul: 'Comfort one another, and edify one another' (1 Th 5:11)" (*Insegnamenti*, V/1, p. 216).

The last element in "spiritual ecumenism" is *prayer, both private and public*, for unity. The Holy Father connects this especially with hope. "Our hope should express itself with a certain boldness, especially the prayer of the Church of Rome and of its bishop, as well as the prayers of all those who are in charge of helping me in my ministry for the universal Church and its unity. This Church, 'founded and established by the two most glorious Apostles, Peter and Paul' must make sure that its fidelity in the service of unity should go hand in hand with the intensity and the confidence of its prayer for unity." This prayer "should be the humble and sincere echo of the prayer of our Lord: 'that all may be one, as Thou, Father, art in Me and I in Thee, that they may all be made one in us' " (Jn 17:21 in *Insegnamenti*, VII, p. 214ff.).

Besides uniting us with the prayer of Christ, our prayer for unity unites us also with that of so many other Christians. "Thus, sharing in this prayer of Christ we also join with so many Christians who, all over the world, despite our divisions, join with Christ in asking for the great grace of that unity which he so ardently desired, and which his power alone can bring about" (*ibid.*). This union of prayer with other Christians is already a great gift and a motive for hope: "The fact that Christians pray together in this way is already in itself a grace and a guarantee of future graces" (*ibid.*).

From spiritual ecumenism let us go on to ecumenism in action. The general idea is that Christians should show the unity which already exists among them. "We can and must immediately reach out and display to the world our unity in proclaiming the mystery of Christ, in revealing the divine dimension as well as the human dimension, of the Redemption; and in struggling with unwearying perseverance for the dignity that each human being has reached and can continually reach in Christ" (*Redemptor*

Hominis, 11). Again, "The seeking for unity and ecumenical concern are a necessary dimension of the Church's whole life. . . . Engaged with our brothers and sisters of the other Churches and ecclesial communities in the ecumenical movement. . .we need to show in all things an anxiety to provide what our Christian brethren legitimately desire and expect from us, knowing their way of thinking and their sensibility. We need, therefore, to develop still more collaboration, so as to attain a more effective service in the cause of unity. The gifts of each one should be developed for the utility and advantage of all" (*Insegnamenti*, VIII/1, p. 1991).

This ecumenism in action, this working together, constitute a common witness given to Christ and to the gospel. On this point the pope insists very energetically: "Above all, we must always be more docile to the Holy Spirit, and to how the Spirit speaks to the Churches today. In all things we need—wherever possible—to show our concern for giving testimony together to Christ and to his gospel, in our world of today which offers us such rich possibilities, but which is also afflicted with so many evils that corrupt it and undermine it. Think of hunger, of the drug plague, of jobless youth. Then there are all the fields in which Christians have much to say, where together they can, through common effort, bring about a reaffirmed respect for human persons, for their moral greatness which today is attacked on all fronts, for humanity's continual advance towards liberty, progress and peace" (*ibid.*, VIII/1, p. 1998).

Naturally, the mission of the Church encounters massive opposition in today's world. Hence the great imperative of the moment for Christians is to join hands "in the noble mission of revealing Christ to the world, of helping each person find himself in Christ, and bringing the contemporary generation of our brothers and sisters, peoples, nations, states, mankind, developing countries and opulent countries—in short, bringing everyone to know 'the unsearchable riches of Christ,' since these riches are for every individual and are everybody's property" (*Redemptor Hominis*, 11).

This collaboration may be extended, within certain limits, even to the field of catechesis itself, as the pope explains in his encyclical *Catechesi Tradendae*: "In situations of religious plurality, the Bishops may consider it opportune or even necessary, to favor certain experiences of collaboration in the field of catechesis between Catholics and other Christians, complementing the normal catechesis that must in any case be given to Catholics. Such experiences have a theological foundation in the elements shared by all Christians" (#33).

His teaching on the duty of laboring for unity is very clear and very rich. "It is certain that in the present historical situation of Christianity and the world, the only possibility we see of fulfilling the Church's universal mission, with regard to ecumenical matters, is that of seeking sincerely, perseveringly, humbly and also courageously, ways to draw closer and to promote union. Pope Paul VI gave us his personal example in this. We must, therefore, seek unity without being discouraged at the difficulties that can arise or accumulate along the road; otherwise we would be unfaithful to the word of Christ, we would fail to accomplish His testament" (*Redemptor Hominis*, 6). In fact, the unity given by Christ to the Church must be "continuously made operative by the community which is called to have 'one heart and one soul' (Acts 1:14). This community knows that the gift it has received 'is carried in earthen vessels' (2 Cor 4:7), and throughout all the Church's history she must never cease watching over it" (*Insegnamenti*, VIII/1, p. 1989).

The pope, however, underscores right away the duties incumbent on all the particular Churches. "Every particular Church, every Bishop, should be concerned about unity, and should promote the ecumenical movement. The new Code of Canon Law, recently promulgated, states this in very clear terms, because such is the will of Christ" (cf. Canon Law 755).

In this connection the pope repeats the necessity for close collaboration among all those directly responsible for ecumenism. "I am pleased to hope that those who are more directly in charge of promoting unity—the ones responsible for ecumenism in the dioceses, the ecumenical commissions of Episcopal Conferences, the Secretariat for the Unity of Christians in the framework of the Roman Curia, all of whom I here wish to congratulate publicly—should be closely associated in a fruitful collaboration" (*Insegnamenti*, III/1, p. 1890).

If the pope speaks of those who are "directly responsible" this does not do away with the fact that the restoration of unity concerns all the members of the Church. "Everyone should collaborate fervently and humbly in this restoration of unity, depending on the responsibilities incumbent on him in the Church" (*ibid.*, III/2, p. 1825). "While we pray for unity, we must feel ourselves very strictly dependent on the Spirit himself.

In him all of us form a single body; and in the exercise of the various ministries entrusted to us, we must all, from first to last, realize that we are an integral part of a grand design of union; we must spend ourselves in silence, in obedience, in sacrifice, even in the most humble duties, because we are sure that our work, like a seed deposited in fertile soil, will give its fruit in the proper time" (*ibid.*, IV/1, p. 144). "Being Christians in our day means being builders of communion in the Church and in society" (*Slavorum Apostoli*, 27).

Obviously, the universal duty of all the members of the Church presupposes an ecumenical training that corresponds with the specific responsibilities of each individual. In general terms we may say: "It is obvious that this new stage in the Church's life demands of us a faith that is particularly enlightened, profound, and responsible. True ecumenical activity means openness, drawing closer, availability for dialogue, and shared investigation of the truth in the full evangelical and Christian sense, but in no way does it, or can it, mean giving up or in any way obscuring the treasures of divine truth that the Church has constantly confessed and taught" (*Redemptor Hominis*, 6).

A specific training is required also for the ones responsible for the ecumenical commissions. To accomplish their task "they need a renewed dedication to ecumenical formation. This presupposes a clear understanding of the Catholic principles governing ecumenism, their full assimilation, along with knowledge of other Churches and ecclesial communities, and of the history of the ecumenical movement" (*Insegnamenti*, VIII/1, p. 1992).

To prepare the faithful for their responsibility it is of fundamental importance that all of our catechesis should have an ecumenical dimension, as the encyclical *Catechesi Tradendae* explains in #32. Here are the main points:

> 1. Catechesis cannot remain aloof from this ecumenical dimension, since all the faithful are called to share, according to their capacity and place in the Church, in the movement towards unity.

> 2. Catechesis will have an ecumenical dimension if—while not ceasing to teach that the fullness of revealed truth and of the means of salvation instituted by Christ is found in the Church—it does so with sincere respect, in words and in deeds, for the ecclesial communities that are not in perfect communion with the Church.

3. In this context, it is extremely important to give a correct and fair presentation of the other Churches and ecclesial communities that the Spirit of Christ does not refrain from using as means of salvation.

4. Catechesis will have an ecumenical dimension if, in addition, it creates and fosters a true desire for unity. This will be true especially if it inspires serious efforts — including the effort of self-purification, in humility and fervor of the spirit, in order to clear the ways — with a view not to facile irenics made up of omissions and concessions on the level of doctrine, but to perfect unity when and by whatever means the Lord will wish.

5. Finally, catechesis will have an ecumenical dimension if it tries to prepare Catholic children and young people, as well as adults, for living in contact with non-Catholics, affirming their Catholic identity while respecting the faith of others.

The pope's ecumenical teaching points out two more important qualities which should characterize our ecumenical effort: patience and confidence. *Patience*: "We must also keep in mind that the path to unity, precisely because it is based on truth and love, requires of all, and especially on the part of public opinion, a deep sense of patience. Some may have gotten the impression that the initial thrust has been blunted." On the contrary, the movement is going forward continuously. "Patience does not mean inaction or resignation; it takes into account the persevering effort which is continually being made, even if, 'hoping against hope' sometimes, but without ever growing discouraged, still forging ahead in the light of the gospel teaching about the grain of wheat which germinates and grows, following the stages willed by God" (*Insegnamenti*, VIII/1, p. 1995).

The passage just cited shows us the intimate connection between patience and *confidence*. In referring to this the pope points out the example of the confidence with which the first Christians went about their immense task in the Roman Empire. "It is true that we must be humble, all the more so because of the wretchedness, the weakness, the selfishness, the injustice still to be found in us too. Humble, yes; but never resigned! Never discouraged! Never inactive! The first Christians did not let themselves be delayed by similar considerations, even though they seemed to be few in number and scattered throughout the immense Roman Empire which had other customs" (*ibid.,* III/2, p. 1831). Elsewhere, the pope indicates the unfailing foundation of this confidence: the power of the Risen Lord. "The communion which we already experience and the full communion for which we pray, are signs of the power of the Risen Lord and of the miracles which his grace can still perform. In this power of the Risen Lord lies the source of our unshakable confidence" (*ibid.,* V/1, p. 215).

Let us conclude with two thoughts which underscore the magnitude and the urgency of the ecumenical tasks facing us.

Referring to the Christian East, the pope affirms: "The dawn of the coming century must find us united in full communion" (*ibid.,* III/1, p. 1889).

Referring to all Christians in the encyclical on the Holy Spirit, John Paul II says: "Of course, we unfortunately have to acknowledge the fact that the millennium which is about to end is the one in which there have occurred the great separations between Christians. All believers in Christ, therefore, following the example of the Apostles, must fervently strive to conform their thinking and acting to the will of the Holy Spirit, 'the true principle of the Church's unity,' so that all who have been baptized in the one Spirit in order to make up one body may be brethren joined in the celebration of the same Eucharist, 'a sacrament of love, a sign of unity, a bond of charity' " (*Dominum et Vivificantem,* 62).

And now, let us go back to *hope.* The Holy Father proposes "a sign of hope" for all those who labor to restore full unity among all the baptized. Recalling the Russian icon of the "Virgin of the Cenacle" in prayer with the Apostles awaiting the Holy Spirit, he asks himself, and us too: "Could she not become the sign of hope for all those who, in fraternal dialogue, wish to deepen their obedience of faith?" (*Redemptoris Mater,* 33).

Jan Cardinal Willebrands
President of the Secretariat
for the Unity of Christians

(Translated from Italian by Richard Arnandez, FSC)

NOTES

1. Cf. Conciliar Decree on Ecumenism: *Unitatis Redintegratio*, 1.

2. I should like to draw attention especially to what, with reference to the Oriental Churches "in quasi total communion" with the See of Rome, has so far been defined: the theological dialogue and the dialogue of charity.

The former, entrusted to the specialists of both Churches, examines in full scientific rigor the causes and the reasons (theological, historical, and so on,) which provoked the break-off of communion between the See of Rome and that of Constantinople, and, consequently of the various Orthodox Churches. The latter has to do with all the contacts, official or not, which are taking place regularly to reaccustom the Churches to live together, to forge closer reciprocal relationships. Few people know, for instance, that the pope regularly sends messages to all the heads of the other Churches and Christian communities at Easter time; or that these Churches through the Secretariat for the Unity of Christians, are kept informed about the most important events or documents emanating from the Catholic Church. Bishops, Metropolitans, leaders of the various Churches have, in the past twenty-five years, established numerous contacts with Rome. In these pages mention is often made of the Second Vatican Council, but let us not forget that observers from the other Churches were present at the extraordinary Synod held in 1985. During these years I myself have frequently represented the Holy Father in world assemblies held by other Churches. Very often we have welcomed groups of Orthodox faithful, Anglicans, Lutherans, members of the Reformed Church, and so on, who had come in order to find out more about the Catholic Church from closer range. Just a few days ago the Bishop Primate of the Evangelical Lutheran Church in America came to visit the Holy Father and the Roman Church, to renew his commitment towards the unity of Christians. For the past eight years a Catholic Sister has been collaborating with the Ecumenical Council of Churches in Geneva, working in the section which deals with mission and evangelization. These are but a few examples, purposely selected at random, to show at least by touching a few high points, how much reality is included in the expression "ecumenical movement."

3. AAS 1985, pp. 1158-59.

4. The Secretariat for Unity was created on June 5, 1960 by John XXIII who gave it the form of a Commission charged with preparing for the Council. The *Motu Proprio*: *Appropinquante Concilio* dated August 6, 1962, confirmed it as a Conciliar organism. In 1963 Pope John XXIII decided that it would include two sections, one for the East, and one for the West. Finally, on August 15, 1967, the apostolic constitution *Regimini Ecclesiae Universae* issued by Paul VI, specified

its aims and its areas of competence for the promoting of unity among Christians.

5. Cf. the same in *Evangelii Nuntiandi*, 77, by Paul VI.

6. Quoted by Augustine Bea in *Ecumenismo nel Concilio*, Milan, 1968.

7. Let us recall in passing that through the Secretariat for the Unity of Christians the Catholic Church carries on a theological dialogue with the Orthodox Church as a whole, with the Anglican Communion, with the World Lutheran Federation, with the World Alliance of Reformed Churches, with the World Methodist Council, with the Pentecostals, with the Disciples of Christ, with the Baptists, and with the Evangelicals. A commission for dialogue with the ancient Oriental Churches is being set up. Further, we need to keep in mind the pluriconfessional dialogue that has taken place in the sphere of worldwide organisms, such as the Ecumenical Council of Churches.

8. Paul VI, AAS, 58, (1966) pp. 60-64.

9. Secretariat for Unity, 38/1978 III-IV.

10. The pope went to Istanbul on November 29, 1979, the day on which the Ecumenical Patriarchate celebrates the feast of its patron St. Andrew. It is perhaps known that for several years, delegations of the Catholic Church have gone to Istanbul for this occasion, and that in return delegations from the Ecumenical Patriarchate journey to Rome for the feast of Saints Peter and Paul on June 29. This is another example of that "dialogue of charity" which I mentioned above.

11. I recall, for instance, with sentiments of gratitude to the Lord, the meeting of the pope on September 11, 1987, with the leaders of other Churches at Columbia University, during his apostolic visit to the United States. It was a moment of great fraternity and deep sharing.

12. The Greek Orthodox Metropolitan of Switzerland, Damaskinos, later preached in St. Peter's, but the Holy Father was not present, for he had, shortly before this, met with an attempt on his life. The circumstance to which we allude here took place during the celebrations called by the Holy Father on the occasion of the 1600th anniversary of the Council of Constantinople, and the 1550th of the Council of Ephesus (June 1988).

13. The citations which follow, taken from the volumes of *Insegnamenti di Giovanni Paolo II* are given within parentheses in the text, under the simple mention of *Insegnamenti*.

THE RELIGIOUS SENSE OF MAN

Joseph Cardinal Cordeiro

1. In his excellent book, *The Ascent of Man*, J. Bronowski has an opening chapter entitled "Less Than the Angels." With such a scriptural ring about it, one would have thought that the author would have taken us to Genesis. Instead, one finds oneself suddenly in the Rift Valley in Kenya, from where he begins to trace the evolution of man. The rest of the book is a stimulating record of man's achievements on earth, but the reference to God is conspicuous by its absence.

This, it seems to me, is typical of today's prevalent atmosphere. Man is so keen on his material advancement that he forgets his true origin and destiny. Pope John Paul II expresses this neatly when he says:

"A critical analysis of our contemporary civilization reveals that in the last century, especially, it has contributed as never before to the multiplication of material goods; but has also created, in theory and especially in practice, a series of attitudes which, more or less notably, display a lessened sensitiveness for the spiritual dimension of human existence" (to the General Assembly of the United Nations, October 2, 1979).

At the heart of his thinking is that man from birth possesses a sense of the Absolute, for Whom he is destined. This is what we call the "religious sense of man," taken individually or as a people. In the course of ten years of catechesis, Pope John Paul II never tires of emphasizing this point, and he does so by considering every aspect of man's being: man individually or collectively, man the creature or conqueror of the universe, man a believer of one religion or in relation to other religions, man the scientist or the man of culture, man at work or at recreation, man a sinner and suffering, or reconciled, man the educator, the vindicator of human rights and religious freedom. The pope seems to have left nothing untouched about man, considered in his relationship with the Absolute. It is from this standpoint that I shall examine in detail what Pope John Paul II has said in the past decade.

To speak of the religious sense of the people, or to speak of the religious sense of man, is for me the same thing. But it does not mean the phenomenon known as "popular religiosity." Nor is my aim directed mainly at examining ecumenical relations in the wider sense of the term, either as comparative religion or religious anthropology. Mine is strictly to examine what Pope John Paul II has said about the innate sense of the Absolute; that is, the religious sense in the human being.

Like Shakespeare, Pope John Paul likes to compare the world to a stage, with man in the center, but man in his relation to God. This, I would say, makes his entire approach anthropotheological:

"With the passing of time, it becomes evident that it is necessary to return over and over again to *the central issue of the world*, which is *man*; man as a creature and child of God" (speech, New Delhi, February 2, 1986).

Throughout his pontificate, this theme is strikingly evident, and I might add that it dominates the early years of his pontificate. This probably is the reason why in these early years is found a constant return to the creation of man and the Book of Genesis.

Pilgrim of the Absolute

2. The religious sense in man derives from the fundamental questions that he asks himself: "Where do I come from? Where am I going?"

"In the unfailing and necessary reflection that man, in any age, is impelled to make about his own life, two questions come strongly to the fore, an echo as it were of God's voice: 'Where do we come from? Where are we going?' " (general audience, January 8, 1986).

To answer these questions, man is forced to reflect. In the process he admits the omnipotence of God in the words of Job:

"After God displayed to Job His divine creative power (cf. Jb 83:41) the latter answered the Lord, saying: 'I know now that Thou canst do all things, and that nothing is impossible for Thee. . . I had known Thee by hearsay, but now my eyes behold Thee' (42:5). May our reflections on creation lead us to the discovery that in the act of creating the world and man God gave us a first and universal testimonial to his all-powerful love, the first prophecy in the history of our salvation" (general audience, January 1, 1986).

Man bears in himself, therefore, the seed of God's universal love. Man's life is God's loving gift. It is a gift at every stage of his existence; but a gift does not lead nowhere—it establishes a relationship with the Giver, a relationship which demands a return. Man's return of love to God is the heart of his religious sense:

"The fact that man is made 'in the image and likeness of God' means, among other things, that he is capable of receiving God's gift; that he is aware of this gift, and that he can respond to it. Precisely for this reason God, from the beginning, established an alliance with man, and with man alone. The Book of Genesis reveals to us not only the natural order of existence, but at the same time, and from the beginning, the supernatural order of grace. We can speak of grace only if we admit the reality of God's gift" (general audience, December 13, 1978).

In this sense man becomes a "pilgrim all his life, a pilgrim of the Absolute, travelling towards a goal, seeking the face of God" (February 1, 1986).

As a pilgrim, man searches. The search for God is his entire being. He must enjoy a freedom of spirit to inquire. To deny him this privilege would be to offend man's dignity. This makes it clear how the search for God must bring out in man the religious sense:

"Is it possible to philosophize about what is 'substantially human' without referring to the complete experience of man? Who has a right to affirm that this full experience of man is to be found in the slogan 'Seek nothing above thyself'? Who has the right to affirm that the full development of man is attained by what closes that experience, and not, instead, by its opening out onto that 'Seek beyond thyself'?" (general audience, January 7, 1979).

Pope John Paul is equally insistent that man's search for God, and consequently his religious sense, is not expressed singly, but jointly with others. Created to the image and likeness of God, man is not alone. The very first chapter of the Book of Genesis makes it clear that God created a communion of persons, and it was this communion of persons that reflected the likeness of God. It is as a communion of persons, therefore, that man must seek God and search for the truth:

"The word 'communion' states more, and with greater precision, because it indicates precisely that 'help' which springs, in a certain sense, from the very fact of existing as a person 'side by side' with another person. In this way. . .we can then deduce that man has become the 'image and likeness of God,' not only through his own humanity, but also through this communion of persons which man and woman formed from the beginning" (general audience, November 14, 1979).

Man's religious sense is therefore expressed by the joint praise that he gives to God in his entire being, unlike every other animal that God has created. Such animals have no heart and mind, they remain closed in their relationships with one another, but man has a heart and mind in the image and likeness of God, and therefore he praises God almost like a priest of creation. The pope expresses this eloquently thus:

"Man's task in the world, therefore, is 'to make life more human and to render the whole earth submissive to this goal' (*Gaudium et Spes*, 38). In this sense man is lord of all material reality. Indeed, he is the 'priest' of the cosmos, whose duty it is to proclaim, in the name of all creatures, the adorable greatness of the Almighty and to give the entire universe back to the Creator as a pleasing sacrifice" (homily at Ordination Mass in Ershad Stadium, Dacca, November 19, 1986).

Worshippers of God

3. Worship of the Absolute is bound to lead to deeper reflection and prayer. Man thus arrives at certain truths or principles which he feels urged to communicate to others. After a certain process, perhaps he may win acceptance from others; new disciples in their turn will begin to propagate his teachings — a new religion is born. There is no need to deny that such a religion is objectivization of man's fundamental religious experience, an exteriorization of his interior longings and attitudes. It is what St. Thomas calls the "*instinctus Dei invitantis*." The world knows many religions, some ancient, some new. As a leader of a world religion himself, Pope John Paul II has been invited sometimes to speak to others:

"His Majesty the King did me the honor of visiting me in Rome some years ago, and he had the courtesy to invite me to visit your country and meet you. I joyfully accepted the invitation from the Sovereign of this country, to speak with you in this Year of Youth" (Morocco, August 19, 1985).

But in his other pastoral journeys, he has also sought the occasions to speak to representatives of non-Christian religions, especially in countries where the predominant religion has been non-Christian and his own flock has been only a *"pusillus grex."*

In every case the pope has pleaded for dialogue and harmony, but it is the basis of this appeal that matters to us, because this basis is the religious sense of the people:

"The Catholic Church recognizes the truths that are contained in the religious traditions of India. This recognition makes true dialogue possible" (Madras, February 5, 1986).

As a pilgrim of the Absolute, this common religious sense offers a noble spiritual vision, inviting him to find the transcendent, and here the pope quotes Mahatma Gandhi:

"What I want to achieve — what I have been striving and pining to achieve — is self-realization — to see God face to face. I live and move and have my being in pursuit of this goal" (*Autobiography,* p. 4-5).

The Holy Father equally and consistently invokes this spiritual vision in man to build up a defense against distress, evil and depression in the world:

"Despite all the powerful forces of poverty and oppression, of evil and sin in all their forms, *the power of truth, will prevail* — the truth about God, *the truth about man*" (Delhi, February 2, 1986).

The evils of this world do nothing to support the dignity of man; on the contrary, they offend it, so it is only when the spiritual vision of man is held in honor and pursued that true liberation of man will be brought about, as also the elimination of all that militates against human dignity.

Here the pope aptly quotes his predecessor, Pope Paul VI:

"There is no true humanism but that which is open to the Absolute and is conscious of a vocation which gives human life its true meaning. . . . Man can only realize himself by reaching beyond himself" (Delhi, February 2, 1986).

Not only against the evils of the world, but against materialism and atheism too, does the pope offer the religious sense in man as a bulwark:

"Your overwhelming sense of the primacy of religion and of the greatness of the Supreme Being has been a powerful witness against a materialistic and atheistic view of life" (Madras, February 5, 1986).

The pope goes further and shows his appreciation of this religious spirit which exists in many cultural traditions:

"You are the heirs and the keepers of an ancient wisdom. This wisdom in Japan and in the Orient has inspired high degrees of moral life. It has taught you to venerate the pure, transparent and honest heart. It has inspired you to discover the divine presence in every creature, and especially in every human being" (Tokyo, 1981).

He pleads that man and society together must try to transcend themselves and seek to foster the spiritual values that are in their soul (Korea, May 6, 1984).

I would be making a serious omission if I did not refer in this context to Pope John Paul's many encounters with Islam. In a talk to youth in Morocco, much appreciated by all, the pope makes three striking points: (1) the mystery of God is the basis of all life; (2) obedience to the mystery leads to a respect for one another; (3) it is the spiritual life in man which has to be developed to seek fulfillment:

"The mystery of God, is it not the highest reality from which depends the very meaning which man gives to his life? And is it not the first problem that presents itself to a young person, when he reflects upon the mystery of his own existence, and on the values which he intends to choose in order to build his growing personality?

"Furthermore, this obedience to God and this love for man should lead us to respect man's rights, these rights which are the expression of God's will and the demands of human nature such as it was created by God.

"Man has need to develop his spirit and his conscience. This is often lacking to the man of today. . . . Man is a spiritual being. We, believers, know that we do not live in a closed world. We believe in God. We are worshippers of God. We are seekers of God" (Morocco, August 19, 1985).

Education, culture, religion

4. To speak of religion without reference to culture would be to omit an important dimension of the *sensus religiosus*; in fact,

the two grow together: "Education, culture, religion grow together" (March 9, 1986).

This applies to all cultures, those which are in advanced societies, and those which are termed "aboriginal." Of the first, the pope's references are ample in his discourses, like in India, Pakistan or Japan. With reference to the aboriginal cultures, however, the Holy Father's talk in Australia on November 29, 1986, is beautifully illustrative of the theme of this essay:

"But for thousands of years you have lived in this land and fashioned a culture that endures to this day. And during all this time, the Spirit of God has been with you. Your 'Dreaming,' which influences your lives so strongly that, no matter what happens, you remain forever people of your culture, is your own way of touching the mystery of God's Spirit in you and in creation. You must keep your striving for God and hold on to it in your lives.

"You live your lives in spiritual closeness to the land, with its animals, birds, fishes, water-holes, rivers, hills, and mountains. Through your closeness to the land you touched the sacredness of man's relationship with God, for the land was the proof of a power in life greater than yourselves.

"The silence of the Bush taught you a quietness of soul that put you in touch with *another world, the world of God's Spirit*" (Australia, November 29, 1986).

Unfortunately, in many parts of the world, man, despite his so-called cultural development, has lost the sense of the religious. We have already referred to the pope's comment on this, in general, about the contemporary society. More particularly, the pope speaks in the same way about Christianity:

"We must admit, realistically and with profound and painful sensitiveness, that today Christians to a large extent feel themselves bewildered, confused, perplexed, and in fact disillusioned. People have spread abroad with profusion ideas that contradict that revealed truth which has always been taught" (to the members of the convention of "Missionaries to the People for the 80's"; February 6, 1981).

And even more particularly he refers to the same phenomenon with regard to Europe:

"It is extremely significant to examine the change undergone by the European mind in this last century. Europe today is shot through by currents, ideologies and ambitions which claim to be extraneous to faith when they do not directly oppose Christianity.

But it is interesting to note how, starting from systems and choices which aimed at making absolute values out of man and his earthly conquests, people have today begun to discuss man himself, his dignity and his intrinsic values, his eternal certitudes and his thirst for the absolute. Where, today, are the pompous proclamations of a certain scientism which pretended to open up before man infinite vistas of progress and well-being? Where are the hopes that man, once having proclaimed the death of God, would finally put himself in God's place in the world and in history, thus inaugurating a new era in which, all by himself, he would overcome all his deficiencies?" (*Insegnamenti*, IV/3, 692).

To redress the balance and make culture once again the vehicles of the religious sense, the pope gives healthy advice both to the Church and to governments. To the Church in particular he advises the evangelization of human culture, so as to return to man a total vision which embraces the spiritual:

"I am firmly convinced that this dialogue between the Church and culture is of great importance for the future of mankind. There are two main and complementary aspects of the question that correspond to the two dimension in which the Church acts. One is the dimension of the evangelization of cultures and the other is that of the defense of man and his cultural advancement" (Korea, May 5, 1984).

"This conception of culture is based on a total vision of man, body and spirit, person and community; a rational being uplifted by love. Yes, the future of man depends on culture. Yes, the peace of the world depends on the primacy of the Spirit. Yes, the peaceful future of humanity depends on love" (*Insegnamenti*, IV/1, 543).

"Dear friends, I cannot fail to speak to you about the primacy of spiritual values in all the areas of the cultural environment in which you live and work, and to which you contribute so significantly. Without spiritual values man is no longer true to himself, because without them he denies or ignores his essential relationship of dependence on the very source of his existence, on his Creator in Whose image he was made and continues to exist" (Nigeria, 1981).

5. In addressing educators, the thrust of the pope's discourse is nearly always to exhort them to draw out the religious sense in all human beings and to develop it as much as possible to the full. With his own university background, the pope is eminently qualified to speak to State and Church universities. But as the pope, he extends his vision to take in theological faculties and every other form of educational institution. In particular he force-fully emphasizes the meaning of higher education in itself, and points out the distinct responsibility that centers of learning have, to develop the religious sense in man.

Education embraces the whole man. It is aimed at promoting and realizing a better harmony between faith and reason at all levels of education. In short, it is the purpose of the university to know God in man, and to know man in God:

"The Catholic University! It should find its ultimate and deepest meaning in Christ, in his message of salvation which embraces man in his total reality, and in the teaching of the Church.

"What must be done is to promote and to bring about in both professors and students an ever more harmonic synthesis between faith and reason, between faith and culture, between faith and life. Such a synthesis must be sought not only on the level of research and of teaching, but also on the pedagogical and educational level. We must seek to know God in man, and to know man in God" (*Insegnamenti*, II/1, 312; and IV/1, 204).

Continuing along this line, the Holy Father draws out at length the meaning of "academe," namely, the mystery of man: man as the image and likeness of God; man looking up to the altar of truth in the expression of his own incompleteness. Here is the act of praise that emanates from the *sensus religiosus*. Thus:

"Scholarship is ultimately theo-centric, because the great nobility of the human mind is based, above all, on its ability to know God and to search more and more deeply into the mystery of God's life, and there at that point to discover also man. Thus the truth of man leads us to the truth of God" (Australia, November 26, 1986).

If all the above applies so aptly to scholarship in general, it is even more applicable to theologians. The pope calls them "specialists of God":

"If this is true for every form of scientific research, it shows itself all the more true for theological investigations, which are bound up with the infinite mystery of God who has communicated himself to us personally, through the word, and the work of Redemption" (October 5, 1979).

The mystery of the Redemption has made man a new creature, and it is for theologians to bring out what the pope calls the "ethos" of this mystery. In this way he will be bringing out the true innate happiness of man in his relation to God:

"In the new creation which is the Redemption, man is assimilated to the image of the only begotten Son; he is freed from sin which marred the beauty of his original being. The ethos of the Redemption is rooted in this redemptive act, and continually draws its power from it. This power places man in a position where he can know and welcome the truth about his own relationships with God and with other creatures. Thus, he is made free to accomplish 'the good works which God has set forth in order for us to practice them.' The ethos of the Redemption is the encounter, in man, of truth with liberty. Saint Augustine wrote: 'the happiness of life lies in the enjoyment of the truth; that is, in the enjoyment of Thee who art the Truth.' The ethos of the Redemption is precisely that happiness" (*Insegnamenti*, VI/2, 70).

The pope is, however, easily able to pass from the sublime to the lowly, from the university professor and graduate to the illiterate uneducated peasant. Literacy is situated in the middle of a process of an adaptation of man to the modern technical world. The illiterate thus become victims of a failure to bring about this adaptation. But more important than its utilitarian and practical aspect is the primary call of education to culture, to the process of development of the human person in his relation to others, the development of man's mind and soul, and the reflection of what man is called to do about his life and his transcendent destiny. How carefully, therefore, the pope emphasizes the attention to be paid to primary education, so that man's sense of God may find a possibility of development:

"And how could they fail to be sensitive thereto in the first place, those whose religion makes it a duty for them to show themselves committed to every disadvantaged brother? May God bless all those who will labor at this sharing of the goods of the spirit" (*ibid.*, V/3, 282).

6. That Pope John Paul II is a philosopher and theologian in his own right and speaks with the added grace of office is known to the whole world. But that he can speak so deftly and deeply on scientific subjects must surely be a sign of magisterial inspiration. His teaching on science covering as wide a range as research, space, physics, genetics, energy, and cosmology, brings out amply the fundamental thesis that man's scientific progress is a flowering of his deeply religious sense. In fact, I would venture to say that it is because Pope John Paul II has understood the thesis so well, that he is able to speak so competently and confidently on scientific subjects.

"So, it is not true science which would mask for man the knowledge of God and His mystery. Science, which feels itself the servant, not the mistress, of the truth; which never loses sight of the sense of mystery because it knows that beyond the limited horizons which it can attain by its own means there lie boundless vistas which are lost in that abyss of light which is called God. Such science not only does not preclude Revelation, but rather prepares the way for the Revelation of God's secrets" (*ibid.,* VII/1, 1978).

"Science, in fact, is a total view of man and of his history; it is the harmony of a unifying synthesis between contingent realities and eternal truth. As Vatican II declared, 'culture must aim at the integral perfection of the human person, at the good of the community and of all human society.' For this reason it is necessary to cultivate man's mind so that his faculties of admiration, of intuition, of contemplation may be developed, and that he may become capable of forming personal judgments, of cultivating a religious, moral and social sense. Indeed, culture, which arises from the reasonable and social nature of man constantly needs a just liberty in order to develop, and it should be allowed the legitimate possibility of an autonomous exercise in accordance with its own principles" (*ibid.,* VI/1, 1228-1229).

But perhaps the pope finds himself more at home on this subject, because he is a man of today, and today is the age of science, and man is at the center of this scientific world.

"Today your gaze is directed at the heavens, not only in order to study and contemplate the stars created by God, as was done by the great figures I have just mentioned, but in order to speak of the space probes, space stations, and satellites made by man. I am with you in your work" (*ibid.*, VII/2, 722).

The pope asks, to whom does space belong? In the past it was the object of study through powerful astronomical instruments. Today that space is visited by man, and his machines, the question is forced upon us, to whom it belongs. The answer is that it belongs to man, but as a gift of God for which man innately thanks him, and should use for peace:

"In your scientific researches and technological inventions, I invite you to seek the God of peace, the Invisible One Who is the source of everything that is visible. I exhort you to seek him by listening to the silence of space. Heaven and earth proclaim that they are only creatures, and they urge you to rise into the supreme heaven of transcendence, in order to open your minds and hearts to the love that moves the sun and the other stars" (*ibid.*, 725).

In an address to mark the centenary of the birth of Albert Einstein, a convention was held on the problem of the cosmos. The pope has this to say:

"Cosmology is a science of totality, of all that exists and is observable, but more because totality itself leads to the Pantocreator.

"Cosmology is the science of totality, of all that exists and is experimentally observable. Hence it is endowed with its own particular epistemological law, which places it perhaps more than any other study in close proximity to philosophy and to religion, because the science of totality spontaneously leads to the question about totality itself, a question which does not find its answer within such totality" (*Insegnamenti*, II/2, 401).

The pope professes that he is even more at home with physics:

"At Krakow, I always sought out and found most fruitful, contacts with the scientific world, and especially with the experts in physical science" (*ibid.*, II/1, 746).

The works of modern physics have tremendous consequences; discoveries have led to nuclear fusion, astrophysics, and the light of synchrotrons. All these discoveries represent in a way the peak of human knowledge, but the knowledge of the world is itself a participation in the science of the Creator:

"Man's knowledge of the world is a way of sharing in the Creator's knowledge. It constitutes, therefore, a first degree of man's resemblance with God, an act of respect towards him; for everything that we discover pays homage to the First Truth" (*ibid.,* 748).

Man, therefore, is not to treat the world as a slave, but rather from his heart he has to praise God for it, as St. Francis did in his "Canticle":

"The savant will not, then, treat nature like a slave; but taking his inspiration from Saint Francis of Assisi's 'Canticle of creatures' he will consider it rather as a sister, called to cooperate with him in opening new paths of progress for humanity" (*ibid.,* 78).

Insistently the pope asks, "Does man use the world of science and technology for the good of man, or not?" The answer:

"To give science and technology a positive orientation towards promoting man's good, we must, as has been said, possess a mature soul, a new inspiration for the spirit, a fidelity to the moral norms which regulate man's life" (*ibid.,* 749).

We are still in the world of philosophical values, but to remain here would be to lead to a false humanism. We need to rise above physics and go to metaphysics, which interprets the full significance of being. False humanism eliminates metaphysics, but to eliminate metaphysics is to eliminate the religious sense, and therefore the religious sense in man, and his desire for the transcendent:

"A certain type of humanism founded on an explicit anti-metaphysical premise, which has invaded so many philosophical expressions in modern times, constitutes an intentional effort to dissociate the empirical from the transcendent, the contingent from the absolute; and, in the last analysis, this is an anti-religious undertaking. The crisis of theory and behavior, of morality and law in the modern world, has, among other causes, mainly that attempt to push aside or to eliminate metaphysics, on which is based man's innate aspiration towards the religious sphere" (*ibid.,* III/2, 542).

"The final question about man drives us back to the meta-empirical area, demanding, and hence justifying, metaphysical considerations, and thus opening human thought to the transcendent" (*ibid.,* 543).

7. Though today in the scientific age the pope has much to teach us, I would not doubt that in his heart of hearts the pope is an even greater lover of the arts, and the proof of this is his love for poetry and scenic beauties of the world. It would be a great omission if we did not look for the *sensus religiosus* of the people when he speaks therefore on the arts, drama, poetry, music, and sports. Though speaking with caution, he speaks with simple depth. At a presentation of Milton's "Paradise Lost" set to music by Penderecki, the Holy Father says:

"I must confess that I was profoundly moved. As for the contents, I remember a phrase uttered perhaps even before the War by an artist whom I knew well: 'Every great work of art is religious in its inspiration and in its roots' " (*ibid.*, II/1, 370).

He emphasizes that originality of style and language, though great arts in themselves, are but an invitation for man to ask fundamental questions about himself, as Milton does in "Paradise Lost" when referring to the first chapter of Genesis. It is not just a chronicle of events that matters, but the fundamental expression of man's being. Is not this the religious sense?

"It is not just a chronicle of certain events; we find expressed there the fundamental experience to which man, in his existence, must always come back, notwithstanding the precisions furnished by Biblical hermeneutics on this subject" (*ibid.*).

Further, that Milton's work was put to music by a Pole, causes the Holy Father to allude to the fact that a nation that is deeply religious and artistic can become the matrix of the highest expression of the religious sense.

Akin to music is art. Religious art in particular makes visible the depth of faith in man. Art confesses God and truth:

"The arts glorify God, and while they seek the beautiful they most often find motives for an encounter with the Truth. . .it is important for you to realize this, and to seek this; to always have before your eyes this deep orientation which binds man to the supernatural" (discourse, April 27, 1981).

"Religious art, in this sense, is a great open book, and an invitation to believe in order to understand. Saint Augustine wrote: 'If faith is not meditated on, it is nothing.' "

And finally, sports. The pope rarely misses an opportunity to speak to visiting sportsmen, but he has always something to say. Not only does he exhort sportsmen to think of the ethic and moral values that sports teaches, such as loyalty, generosity, creativity, sacrifice and self-control, but these all lead to the formation of the person, opening man, therefore, to the horizons of transcendence and faith, and even more, it does this by uniting people:

"The formation of the person, thus laid open to wider horizons of transcendence and of faith. . . . While sincerely rejoicing with you I hope that it [sports] may ever favor the links of fraternity between individuals, groups and nations, in harmony with the eloquent motto you have selected, *Ludis jungit*" (March 26, 1981).

The profound reality of man

8. Having seen man at the center of the universe in his relationships with the world and people, and in the ascent of his achievements, it now remains to descend into man himself, and see the basic relationships he has with himself; in his work, suffering, sin, and reconciliation. All these somehow closely form part of man's inner life, and in one way or another express the *sensus religiosus* in him.

Commenting on the Parable of the Workers in the Vineyard (cf. Mt 20:1), the pope emphasizes that man must try to recover the true meaning of work, not only in itself, but especially in the salvific design of God. Through his work, man somehow or other expresses his own sense of the religious:

"In fact, according to God's plans, we must, through our work, not only rule over the earth but also attain salvation. Hence, labor involves not only a temporal dimension, but an eternal one" (Angelus, September 20, 1981).

Work, however, means toil, and often suffering, whether it is personal or social, but man's suffering is not restricted only to his work. Every other form of suffering dogs man's footsteps — physical or spiritual. Today's world has discovered more than ever before how much mental stress and suffering accompany man's life. What is often lost sight of, is that suffering has an interior dimension, which takes man outside of himself to God:

"What we express by the word 'suffering' seems to be particularly essential to the nature of man. It is as deep as man himself, precisely because it manifests in its own way that depth which is proper to man, and in its own way surpasses it. Suffering seems to belong to man's transcendence; it is one of those points in which man is in a certain sense 'destined' to go beyond himself, and he is called to this in a mysterious way" (*Salvifici Doloris*, 2).

This destiny is supernatural, because it is rooted in the mystery of the Redemption of the world. Difficult as it is for man, on account of the pain it involves, the meaning of suffering is truly human and supernatural:

"This is the meaning of suffering, which is truly supernatural, and at the same time, human. It is supernatural because it is rooted in the divine mystery of the Redemption of the world, and it is likewise deeply human because in it, the person discovers himself, his own humanity, his own dignity, his own mission" (*ibid.,* 31).

Suffering, however, came into this world as a result of sin. While man laudably tries to eliminate every form of suffering, he fails often to acknowledge its source, that is, sin. Loss of the sense of sin, rooted in the sense of loss of God, is a feature of contemporary life in many parts of the world. Is not this the loss of the religious sense in man? The Holy Father again and again exhorts us to try to recover this particular religious sense:

"This sense of sin is rooted in man's moral conscience, and is as it were its thermometer. It is linked to the sense of God, since it derives from man's conscious relationship with God as his Creator, Lord, and Father. Hence, just as it is impossible to eradicate completely the sense of God, or to silence the conscience completely, so the sense of sin is never completely eliminated.

"In fact, God is the origin and the supreme end of man, and man carries in himself a divine seed. Hence it is the reality of God that reveals and illustrates the mystery of man. It is therefore vain to hope that there will take root a sense of sin against man and against human values, if there is no sense of offense against God, namely, the true sense of sin" (*Reconciliatio et Paenitentia*, 18).

The pope, however, encourages and reminds us that God does not abandon us. His very nature is love and mercy. Present-day mentality is often unable to realize God's mercy because it is too full of itself. In fact, it is inclined to regard mercy as a relationship of inequality between the Giver and the receiver. Consequently, mercy is looked upon as an offense against the dignity of man.

Pope John Paul clearly and sharply points out the fallacy of this kind of thinking, and thus draws out what is basic in man:

"The present-day mentality, more perhaps than that of people in the past, seems opposed to a God of mercy, and in fact tends to exclude from life and to remove from the human heart the very idea of mercy. The word and the concept of 'mercy' seem to cause uneasiness in man who, thanks to the enormous development of science and technology, never before known in history, has become the master of the earth and has subdued and dominated it" (*Dives in Misericordia*, 2).

"What took place in the relationship between the father and son in Christ's parable is not to be evaluated 'from the outside.' Our prejudices about mercy are mostly the result of appraising them only from the outside. At times it happens that by following this method of evaluation, we see in mercy above all a relationship of inequality between the one offering it and the one receiving it. And, in consequence, we are quick to deduce that mercy belittles the receiver, that it offends the dignity of man. The Parable of the Prodigal Son shows that the reality is different: the relationship of mercy is based on the common experience of the dignity that is proper to him" (*ibid.*, 6). Mercy is the content of intimacy with the Lord.

CONCLUSION

9. After having examined the entire range of Pope John Paul's discourses on the religious sense in man, can we arrive at any possible definition of this religious sense? I find it difficult to do this myself; it is so much a part of the kingdom of God in man, that like the kingdom itself, it defies definition. The most appealing way I could express it would be to say that there is deep down in man a hunger for God. In the very words that the Holy Father used himself when he visited my home town:

"And yet it still remains true that man does not live on bread alone. The human person has necessities which go deeper still; knows a hunger keener yet than that which bread can satisfy. It is the hunger in the human heart for God in all his immensity" (homily at National Stadium in Karachi, February 16, 1981).

It is a hunger which is expressed in all man's relationships, achievements, failures, sin, suffering, and reconciliation. It is rooted in him and cannot be taken away. Let the pope himself have the last word. Commenting on Saint Augustine, "You made us for Yourself, Lord, and our hearts are restless until they rest in You," he says:

"In this creative restlessness beats and pulsates what is most deeply human—the search for truth, the insatiable need for the good, hunger for freedom, nostalgia for the beautiful, and the voice of conscience" (*Redemptor Hominis*, 18).

Joseph Cardinal Cordeiro
Archbishop of Karachi
(Pakistan)

MISSION AND DIALOGUE
IN THE TEACHING OF JOHN PAUL II

Josef Cardinal Tomko

Guided by the Holy Spirit, and attentive to the signs of the times, Pope John Paul II seeks with special insight, constancy, and sensitivity to bring out the deepest nature and the dynamic character of the Church's evangelizing mission. He helps us to rediscover, and of course to understand more profoundly, within ever-widening horizons, the dimensions and the implications of this mission, which seeks, precisely, to enter into a dialogue with that world which the Church is called upon to evangelize.

In these reflections on "Mission and dialogue in the teaching of John Paul II" we shall strive to bring together his manifold observations, more occasional than organic, made during the ten years of his pontificate, and to group them around certain specific points: 1) the nature and purpose of mission activity (its Christological-Trinitarian basis; its purpose in salvation history, and its ecclesial dimension); 2) the persons involved in the mission (the pope, the bishops, priests, missionaries, and lay persons); 3) dialogue, as the instrument and the method of mission activity (evangelization in the first place, dialogue with other religions, dialogue with various cultures, and the promotion of human values).

I. NATURE AND PURPOSE OF MISSIONARY ACTIVITY

The Church realizes that the primary source of her mission, the unwavering foundation and the supreme purpose of her being sent to all peoples, proceed from an eternal and universal plan of salvation springing from the love of the Father, the redemptive action of the Son, and the sanctifying role of the Holy Spirit. So true is this that the Council presents the Church to us as "a people made one with the unity of the Father, Son and Holy Spirit" (*Lumen Gentium*, 4).

1. The Christological-Trinitarian basis of the Church's mission

Thus, the basis of the Church's mission is a trinitarian one. God the Father, "in His immense and merciful benevolence, creates us freely and, moreover, gratuitously calls us to share in His own life and glory" (*Ad Gentes*, 2). The Son, for his part, reveals and actuates in a sublime manner this dialogue of salvation which springs from the "Fount of love" which is the charity of the Father. The Holy Spirit, finally, brings to completion from within this work of salvation, and stimulates the Church towards implementing this activity.

John Paul II, in his encyclical *Dominum et Vivificantem* (1986) speaking of "the Spirit of the Father and of the Son given to the Church" develops in detail this theology of the "intra-trinitarian missions" when he writes: "The Father sends the Holy Spirit in the power of His fatherhood, even as He had sent the Son; but at the same time He sends Him in the power of the redemption accomplished by Christ; and in this sense the Holy Spirit is also sent by the Son. 'I will send Him to you' " (*Dominum et Vivificantem*, 8).

Thus, in the farewell paschal discourse we find not only the summit of trinitarian Revelation, but we are faced by definitive events and by the final words "which, in the end, will be translated into the great missionary mandate addressed to the Apostles, and through them to the Church: 'Go, and make disciples of all nations' " (*ibid.*, 9).

This is why evangelization and the mission are not, for the Church, something optional, supplementary, or marginal. The Church was born as a missionary Church; and by her nature as well as by her origin she is a missionary Church.

From the "intra-trinitarian missions" which constitute the inner mystery of the divine life which is Father, Son, and Holy Spirit in the divine unity of the Trinity, the "mission" of the Church derives its origin; this mission is specified as a task which tends towards making people "capable" of sharing in the inscrutable love of the God who is One in Three.

Moreover, the Church has received from her divine Founder the formal mandate: "Go, and preach the Gospel to all nations, baptizing them in the name of the Father and of the Son and of the Holy Spirit" (Mt 28:19; Mk 16:15).

2. The mission's purpose in salvation history

The task of evangelizing peoples finds its primary origin in God's salvific will. "He wants all to be saved and to come to the knowledge of the truth" (1 Tm 2:4). Since there is no salvation in any other (Acts 4:12) "it is necessary that all should be converted to Christ once they have come to know Him through the preaching of the Church, and that they should be incorporated into Him and into His Church, His body, through baptism" (*Ad Gentes*, 7).

"Hence, although in ways which He alone knows, God can lead those who through no fault of their own remain ignorant of the Gospel, to that faith without which it is impossible to please Him, still it remains the Church's unshirkable task, as well as her most sacred right, to spread the Gospel; thus missionary activity retains, today as always, its necessity and its validity" (*ibid.*).

This is why John Paul II in his address to the Pontifical Missionary Works in May 1986, could say: "If she is not a missionary Church, the Church is not even evangelical" (*Osservatore Romano*, May 14, 1986).

Christ and the Church, then, remain the "ordinary" ways to salvation. Hence no one can minimize either "the necessity of the Church" (*Ad Gentes*, 7) which has been established as the "sign and universal sacrament of this salvation" (*Lumen Gentium*, 48; *Ad Gentes*, 1, 5) or her mission to evangelize, which is the primary means she uses in accomplishing this work of salvation, and the foremost duty of the entire People of God.

John Paul's teaching insists with special emphasis both on the necessity of the mission and on the "sacramental" role played by the Church as the "ordinary" locus of salvation, in reference to other religions.

In a genuinely missionary spirit John Paul II, following the teaching of the Council and of his predecessors — a precious inheritance which he has received and strives to preserve and apply — affirms clearly that "the Church, the depository of the Good News, not only cannot refrain from speaking out, but even today no less than in other times must necessarily send out apostles and missionaries, who are able to speak to mankind of God's transcendent and liberating salvation, thus guiding them — in complete fidelity to the Spirit — to the knowledge of the truth. We must obey the unchanging mandate of our Lord, and hence we must all labor, striving with might and main, no doubt in various ways and with varying types of action, but in an organic and substantial unity of intent, to bring about the proclamation and the diffusion of the Gospel. Yes, my brothers, even though we do not depart for missionary lands, all of us have, and will always have, and must everywhere have the possibility and the obligation of collaborating in this evangelizing activity, which is presented to us as 'the fundamental duty of God's people' (*Ad Gentes*, 35)" (Message for World Mission Day, 1980).

For John Paul II this subject of evangelization is the central and all-absorbing topic, not only when he speaks in the so-called mission lands, but also when he turns to address the churches with a long-standing Christian tradition, such as those in Europe. He reminds the latter that they are called to infuse a soul into modern society, and that they can do this only if they bring about a re-flourishing of a new era of evangelization, which is still today capable of bringing into contact the modern world and the life-giving energy of the gospel. It was precisely in the sixth Symposium of the bishops of Europe that the pope said: "In this perspective of evangelization the whole problem of mission activity needs to be viewed. Up to rather recent times, the abundance of missionary vocations constituted an important dimension in the evangelization of Europe itself. Today, to some extent, this dimension has been weakened, even though it still makes itself felt in its effects. We must understand that it will not be possible to re-inaugurate an effective program of evangelization without reviving the missionary spirit of our Christian communities.

"For this reason, precisely, it must never be forgotten that the primary mission of the Church, under the influence of the Holy Spirit, is to preach and bear witness to the Good News, the happy news of God's choice, of his mercy and love, which are manifested in salvation history; which, through Jesus Christ, comes to complete fruition in the fullness of time, and impart and offer salvation to mankind, in virtue of the Holy Spirit. Christ is the Light of the world" (*Osservatore Romano*, December 10, 1985).

In this way the Church seeks to live fully the urgency and the necessity of the evangelizing mission entrusted to her by her Spouse and Lord. "Mission" thus becomes the proper name of the Church, and in a certain sense constitutes her very definition.

The Church, indeed, becomes her true self only when she accomplishes her mission integrally.

3. The ecclesial dimension of the mission

"The Church, living in time, is by her nature a missionary Church, since it is from the mission of the Son and that of the Holy Spirit that she, in the plan of God the Father, derives her own origin" (*Ad Gentes*, 2). It is in this plan of God concerning all mankind, history, and the world, that the mission of the Church is located—a mission which continues and develops the mission of Christ, at his command, and in the power of his Spirit; this is the task which justifies her very existence and all of her activity.

In the Church, missionary by her very nature, and established as the universal sacrament of salvation "following the impulse given by the Ecumenical Council, and in fidelity to her own purposes, there has arisen an increased desire to understand more deeply the theme of evangelization, both at the level of the universal Church, and at that of the local churches" (*Osservatore Romano*, October 12, 1985).

1. The missionary dimension in the universal Church

On the feast of the Epiphany in 1979, John Paul II said: "The Church is conscious of God's mission which is actuated through her. . . . Mission is the proper name of the Church, and in a certain sense it constitutes her definition. The Church becomes her true self when she accomplishes her mission" (*Insegnamenti*, II, p. 18).

To evangelize, then, is the essential mission, the proper vocation and the deepest identity of the Church, which is, in her turn, evangelized.

Summing up his journey to Africa in May, 1980, John Paul II explained that this missionary consciousness "has become, in a certain sense, a fundamental dimension of the living faith of every Christian, a manner of living of every parish, every religious congregation, and of the various communities" (*ibid.*, III, p. 1419).

Addressing the sixth Symposium of the bishops of Europe, the pontiff pointed out how today we are witnessing a "revival of the missionary ideal of the contemporary world." And he added: "This will be a renewed grace, which will produce fruits of evangelization in proportion as it is directed towards re-discovering the original inspiration of Vatican II, interiorizing it, and pursuing it with renewed fervor and apostolic zest" (*Osservatore Romano*, October 12, 1985).

Hence we can say: the Church, as she has most forcefully repeated to herself, must by the will of her divine Founder be the sign and the instrument of salvation for all humanity. So too she has likewise added that to be capable of fulfilling this role and of corresponding therewith in concrete ways, as she goes through history, she must always have the spirit and the manner, the vigilant attention and the sacred ambition to be and to remain authentically missionary. "The Church's self-definition (to be a missionary Church) is at the same time the proof and confirmation of that self-realization that the Council—that great event of light and grace—brought forth and strengthened within her. It is as though the Holy Spirit had repeated to her: 'know thyself, and be thyself, for thou art, in Christ, the organ of salvation for all nations; so then, be missionary'" (*Insegnamenti*, III/2, p. 918).

Speaking of himself, of his mission and of his missionary travels, John Paul II described it all as marked by this "new consciousness of her mission" that the Church has of herself. He said: "Hence, this has become also a true and adequate means of accomplishing the pastoral role of the Bishop of Rome. It seems that since Vatican II he cannot fulfill his duty in any other way than by going out towards mankind, and hence towards peoples and nations in the spirit of those words in which Christ so clearly ordered his Apostles to go out to all the world and to teach 'all nations, baptizing them in the name of the Father, and of the Son, and of the Holy Spirit' (Mt 28:18)" (*Insegnamenti*, III/1, p. 1419).

2. The missionary role of particular churches

According to that original reference, the Trinity, where different Persons subsist within the unity of God, we also need to view the relationship existing between the universal Church and the particular churches in which, *de facto* it is incarnated. According to the Lord's thinking, it is the same Church which, universal by her mission and vocation, strikes root in various cultural, social, and human terrains, assumes throughout the world external aspects and expressions of different kinds, without losing the missionary root which especially qualifies it as the Church of Christ.

In virtue of this inseparable bond between the universal Church and the particular churches, the universal Church's missionary concern must also be the missionary concern of each particular church.

John Paul II stresses this new awareness present in the Church today when he says: "Every diocese is, therefore, called to become more conscious of this universal dimension, that is, to discover, or re-discover, its own missionary nature, widening the scope of its charity to embrace the boundaries of the world, and demonstrating for those who are afar the same solicitude that it has for those who are its members" (Message for World Mission Day, 1982).

A church, once evangelized, must necessarily become an evangelizing church. Precisely for this reason John Paul II, speaking to the bishops of Ghana at Mumasi, invited that ecclesial community to extend its own "missionary dimension in regard to the needs of its sister churches on the African continent" (*Insegnamenti*, III/1, p. 1267).

In his recent visit to the Latin American continent, which he defined as "a continent of hope," John Paul II said: "As we approach the third millennium of Christianity, America must feel itself called to make its influence bear on the universal Church and in the world, through renewed evangelizing activity, which will show forth the power of Christ's love to all mankind, and will sow Christian hope in so many hearts, thirsting for the living God" (*Osservatore Romano*, October 4, 1987).

And in his message to the third Latin-American Missionary Congress, John Paul II repeated to the Christians of that continent: "America, the hour has struck for you to become evangelizers, and to venture forth beyond your frontiers" (*ibid.*, August 6, 1987).

3. Mary, the "star of evangelization"

John Paul II dedicated the second part of his recent encyclical *Redemptoris Mater* to "the Mother of God, in the midst of the pilgrim Church." In the heart of this pilgrim and missionary Church Mary "is present. . . as the one who advanced on the pilgrimage of faith, sharing, unlike any other creature, in the mystery of Christ" (*Redemptoris Mater*, 25).

By means of that same faith which made her blessed, "Mary is present in the Church's mission, present in the Church's work of introducing into the world the kingdom of her Son" (*ibid.*, 28).

This is why "It is to her, as Mother and Model, that the Church must look in order to understand in its completeness the meaning of her own mission" (*ibid.*, 37).

In every one of his missionary journeys John Paul II never fails to look up to Mary as the perfect "icon" in which is reflected in all its fullness the deep meaning of the Church's missionary being.

In the general audience of May 23, 1979, the pope said: "Let us also pray with insistence and confidence to the most holy Virgin, Queen of the missions, so that she may always make the faithful feel concern for the missions, and their responsibility for the spreading of the gospel.

"Mary, who was present on Pentecost Day when the life of the Church began with the apostles, the disciples, and the holy women, always remains present in the Church. She, the first missionary, is the Mother and support of all those who announce the gospel."

And in his homily at Mass in the Basilica of Our Lady of Aparecida, recalling Mary as the Mother of the Church, as the one who, remaining a virgin, conceived through the action of the Holy Spirit the Word made flesh, John Paul II said: "What is the Church's mission if not to cause Christ to be born in the hearts of the faithful through the action of the same Holy Spirit, and by means of evangelization? Thus, the 'star of evangelization' as my predecessor Paul VI called her, points out and enlightens the paths for the proclamation of the gospel."

II. THE SUBJECTS OF THE MISSION

Since the mission is for the whole Church a constitutive element that cannot be given up, it follows that "all the faithful, as members of the living Christ, have a strict obligation to cooperate in the expansion and growth of His Body, so as to bring Him as soon as possible to His fullness" (*Ad Gentes*, 36).

Consequently, "all the children of the Church must keenly realize their responsibility as regards the word" (*ibid.*). Hence, "given that the entire Church is by her very nature a missionary Church, and that the work of evangelization remains a fundamental duty of the People of God, all the faithful, conscious of their responsibility, must take up their respective share in the missionary work" (Canon Law 781).

However, if all the People of God are responsible for the Church's mission, and all together are its subjects, this is not true in the same way or by the same title for all, but according to the special traits of the ministry, vocation, or charism that each individual has received from God, within that organic communion special to the Church. Nobody possesses these gifts personally in their totality; and no one is deprived of them either, but "they come together with each other and complete each other for the one communion and mission" (*Mutuae Relationes*, 9).

Keeping in mind the missionary character of the whole People of God, John Paul II repeatedly stresses in his teaching the special mission of those who exercise this function as their own particular and specific grace.

1. The pope, herald of the gospel

As the supreme pastor of a Church which is entirely missionary, the pope must be the first missionary, seeking to imitate the example of Christ, "the very first and the greatest evangelizer" (*Evangelii Nuntiandi*, 7) and placing himself under the guidance of the Holy Spirit, "the principal Agent of evangelization" (*ibid.*, 75).

Speaking of this, his unshirkable missionary duty, John Paul II said: "From the start of my pontificate I took to heart the words of Vatican II, where it is said that 'on the successor of Peter was imposed in a special way the great duty of spreading the Christian name' (*Lumen Gentium*, 23). Following the example of my predecessor Paul VI, I set out to visit numerous countries where Christ is scarcely known, or where the gospel proclamation of the mission is still incomplete. My journeys have an eminently religious and missionary purpose. I wished to announce the gospel myself, making myself in some manner an itinerant catechist, and to encourage all those who labor in the service of the gospel. To all I wanted to pay my respects, and to express my gratitude in the name of the universal Church" (Message for World Mission Day, 1981).

In 1980 when visiting the leprosarium of Maritube at Belem, in Brazil, John Paul II said: "I come to you as a missionary sent by the Father and by Jesus, to continue to proclaim the Kingdom of God which begins in this world, but which is fulfilled only in eternity, to strengthen the faith of my brothers and sisters, to create a deep communion among all the children of the same Church" (*Insegnamenti*, III/2, p. 193).

The pope clearly understands that "mission" means the revelation of God's power for the salvation of whoever believes. It is in the context of the urgency of this manifestation that all and every one of the journeys and pilgrimages of the pope assumes their full significance. These journeys are visits paid to each of the local churches, and demonstrate the place that these communities have in the universal dimensions of the Church, and underline the particular role they play in the building up of the Church's universality. As he himself affirmed more than once, every trip he takes is "a genuine pilgrimage to the living sanctuary of the People of God" (*ibid.*, II, p. 765).

Speaking to his collaborators in the central government of the Church on June 28, 1980, the pontiff himself said: "The pope travels, supported, like Peter, by the prayers of the whole Church, to proclaim the gospel, to confirm his brethren in the faith, to consolidate the Church, to meet with men and women. These are journeys of faith, of prayer, which always have in their center meditation on, and proclamation of the word of God, eucharistic celebration, the invocation of Mary. They are so many opportunities for a travelling catechesis, for gospel proclamation, thus prolonging at all latitudes the gospel and the apostolic magisterium, expanded to today's planetary dimensions. These are journeys of love, of peace, of universal brotherhood" (*ibid.*, III/1, p. 1886-87).

How could one fail to recognize in this itinerant missionary solicitude the special charism of today's Petrine ministry on the paths of the world? This is the apostolic method which in John Paul II is expanding to planetary dimensions.

2. The bishops, responsible for the evangelization of the world

The mission confided by Christ to Peter and to the other apostles still continues today in the person of the bishops in union with the Roman pontiff, Vicar of Christ and visible head of the whole Church. Thus, after the Apostolic College with Peter at its head, has followed the Episcopal College with the pope at its head.

It follows that the task of proclaiming the gospel everywhere on earth pertains to the body of pastors, to all of whom in common Christ gave his command, thereby imposing upon them a common duty of preaching the gospel to every creature (cf. *Lumen Gentium*, 23; *Ad Gentes*, 38; *Christus Dominus*, 6). Every bishop, in fact, was ordained not only for a diocese but for the salvation of the whole world (cf. *Ad Gentes*, 38).

In his Message for World Missionary Day in 1982, John Paul II recalling the encyclical *Fidei Donum* of Pius XII, solemnly repeated the principle of the bishops' co-responsibility, by reason of their belonging to the Episcopal College, in the evangelization of the world. He said to them: "To them, as successors of the apostles, Christ has entrusted, and still entrusts, before anyone else, the common mandate of proclaiming and propagating the Good News, even to the ends of the earth. They, therefore, although they are the pastors of individual parts of the flock are, and must feel themselves, responsible in solidarity, in union with the Vicar of Christ, for the progress of the whole Church, and for the fulfilling of her missionary task.

"Hence, every bishop, head and guide of the local church, must bend his energies in this direction; must, that is, do all he can to give a vigorous missionary impulse to his diocese. To him, first of all belongs the duty of creating in the faithful a Catholic mentality in the fullest sense of the word, open to the needs of the universal Church, of making the People of God sensitive to their unescapable duty to cooperate in its various forms. . . of favoring in a very special manner priestly and religious vocations, and at the same time of helping the clergy to acquire a clearer understanding of the typically apostolic dimension of the priestly ministry" (*Insegnamenti*, V/2, 1877-78).

In communion with the successor of Peter, all the bishops "in as much as they are members of the Episcopal College which has succeeded to the Apostolic College" (*Ad Gentes*, 38), must place evangelization as the primary end of their episcopal ministry, and as such they should be masters of the truth, signs and builders of unity, defenders of human dignity, promoters in the light of the gospel of the integral progress of humanity.

3. Missionary role of priests

Collaborators of the bishop with whom they are intimately associated by virtue of their ordination itself, and by their ministry, priests share in the latter's concerns and in his missionary responsibility.

By its very nature, then, "The priestly ministry shares in the same universal extension of the mission entrusted by Christ to the Apostles" (*Presbyterorum Ordinis*, 10).

Speaking to American priests at Philadelphia in 1979 John Paul II said: "The priestly ministry is essentially a missionary one; this means that priests are sent for others, as Christ was sent by his Father, because of the gospel, and to evangelize" (*Insegnamenti*, II/2, p. 602).

The following year, speaking to French priests in Notre Dame, he added: "O apostles of Jesus Christ, by the will of God, preserve that apostolic and missionary solicitude which is so strong in your country. . . . In this pastoral and missionary perspective may your ministry always be that of the apostle of Jesus Christ, of the priest of Jesus Christ. Never lose sight of why you were ordained: to make people advance in divine life" (*ibid.*, III/1, p. 1533).

On the occasion of the twenty-fifth anniversary of the missionary encyclical *Fidei Donum* of Pius XII, John Paul II encouraged especially that concrete form of cooperation which consists in sending diocesan priests to the missions, the so-called *Fidei Donum* priests, in response to the more urgent needs of many churches which suffer from the worrisome shortage of apostles and servants of the gospel.

He said: "This is the great novelty to which *Fidei Donum* has lent its name. A novelty which has led to the transcending of the territorial dimensions of priestly service, to direct it to the whole Church, as the Council stressed: 'The spiritual gift which priests receive at their ordination, prepared them not for a sort of limited and narrow mission, but for the widest possible and universal mission of salvation, even to the ends of the earth; for every priestly ministry shares in the universality of the mission entrusted by Christ to His apostles' " (*De Presbyterorum*, 10).

He then exhorted the bishops to send generously their own priests to those regions which need them most urgently, even if their own dioceses have no oversupply of priests. "It is not a question of making you suffer restrictions to help the others, but to bring about a certain equality. . . . If a poor diocese helps another poor diocese, this cannot bring about a greater impoverishment for the former, because the Lord is never overcome in generosity" (*ibid.*).

John Paul II also pointed out with deft allusions the advantages of this precious form of missionary cooperation. "The benefit of such a ministerial undertaking, even though temporary, is double: the priests who devote themselves thereto not only offer an evident service to the missionary churches; then, when they return to their home dioceses they bring with them the treasure of their experience, and contribute in this way to the task of arousing among the faithful themselves their missionary conscientiousness, and the will to support the cause of evangelization" (World Mission Day Message, 1980).

4. Religious

The Decree on the Missionary Activity of the Church had already spoken about the missionary duty incumbent on religious of both sexes belonging to both active and contemplative communities. It declared that, up to now, "they have had and still have a most important share in the evangelization of the world" (*Ad Gentes*, 40).

John Paul II fully realizes how important is this role of religious, both men and women, in the missions. In his meeting with religious and members of consecrated life in Buenos Aires, Argentina, on April 10, 1987, he had this to say: "The divine call to the religious profession, to the permanent practice of the evangelical counsels, opens new horizons to the Church's apostolic effort, and from this there arise new energies for evangelization. . . . Those who are called to this consecration, and who take their places within the Church's dynamic action, are *par excellence* people who have volunteered to leave all and to go and spread the gospel to the ends of the earth.

"You were called, dear brothers and sisters, to experience within yourselves and to live out in all its consequences the motto of St. Paul which becomes a daily examination of conscience; 'Woe to me, if I do not preach the gospel!' Yes, woe to me, woe to us if we today do not know how to present the gospel to a world which, in spite of appearances, still hungers for God."

During that same journey, at Montevideo, Uruguay, on March 31, 1987, he spoke to the cloistered religious women, and said: "Know, my dearest daughters, that you occupy a privileged place in the heart of the Church, because like St. Teresa of Jesus and so many other contemplative souls, you are, as it were, 'the love in the heart of the Church.' Live with profound joy in the knowledge that through your demanding and austere life you too are evangelizers, with a mysterious and apostolic fecundity."

5. The missionaries

After recalling to mind that the duty of spreading the gospel is binding on every disciple of Christ in proportion to his opportunities, the decree *Ad Gentes* on the missionary activity of the Church affirms that through the Holy Spirit the Lord Jesus also distributes as he wills special charisms for the good of souls. Thus, there springs into place in individual hearts the "missionary vocation" which impels one to take on, as a specific duty, the task of evangelization which refers to the entire Church (cf. *Ad Gentes*, 23).

We must then recognize as a "special vocation" the call of those who are provided with the natural aptitude, and who, thanks to their qualities and talents, feel themselves prepared to undertake missionary activity when mandated by legitimate authority.

Speaking to such missionaries, John Paul II said: "Once again it is a joy for me to praise and to express lively gratitude to the missionaries who, sometimes at the cost of tremendous sacrifices and amidst all kinds of difficulties, sow the seed of the word, from which the Church grows and takes root in the world. And the most consoling fruit of this heroic and infatigable labor of theirs is the marvelous flourishing of young, fervent Christian communities, the soil from which priestly and religious vocations will spring, the hope of the Church of tomorrow.

"Yes, the missionaries are the indispensable workers for the Lord's vineyard, and the local churches of recent foundation, even while developing their native clergy still need the presence and the energies of the missionaries, even for the purpose of enriching themselves with the centuries-old traditions, and with the maturity of the older churches, which the missionaries bring. So it is that between both sorts of local churches there grows up a fruitful exchange of ideas, initiatives, and works, which is like a beneficial osmosis for the universal Church" (*Insegnamenti*, III/1, p. 1483-84).

During his journey to Brazil in 1980, during the homily of his Mass at Manaus, John Paul II said this to the missionaries: "I desire in the first place to urge you on and encourage you in your missionary labors. This is certainly an exacting task. . . . In these difficult moments you should find comfort and courage in the certainty that your labor is not only useful and necessary, but indispensable for building up the Church in this corner of the earth, which, I well know, you have adopted as your own. Finally, I declare with absolute sincerity the immense appreciation that the pope feels for your labors, the respect, admiration and fraternal affection that he entertains for your persons" (*ibid.*, III/2, p. 242).

Reciting the Angelus on World Mission Day in 1982, the pope addressed a special greeting to the select band of missionaries of both sexes throughout the world. He told them: "To these, as to my specially beloved brothers and sisters, along with my greetings and best wishes I send my words of praise, my encouragement and my thanks. These are sentiments which I love to express publicly. And foremost among these sentiments, I must add, is my gratitude, because it is thanks to the work of you missionaries that the Church of Christ, like the power of the good seed and the good leaven in the gospel, increases and spreads" (*ibid.*, V/3, p. 900).

6. The missionary role of lay persons

Coinciding with the Bishops' Synod in 1987, John Paul II published his World Mission Day message, and took advantage of this favorable coincidence to rekindle in the faithful laity, men and women of all ages and conditions, the realization that they belong to a people which is missionary by its very nature. The

Church, in fact, was born missionary, and evangelization is for her the law of life. Citing Vatican II, the pope recalled that "evangelization is not reserved to the hierarchy alone; but every disciple of Christ is bound by the duty of spreading the faith, as far as his station in life permits. And the root of this duty is found in the first of the sacraments of the faith. Thus, all Christian laypersons, precisely in virtue of their baptism, are called by the Lord to an effective apostolate. The Christian vocation, by its very nature, is also a vocation to the apostolate. It is a call founded on the grace of baptism itself; incorporated into Christ through baptism Christians become sharers in Christ's priestly, prophetic, and royal functions. Confirmation strengthens them with the power of the Holy spirit, while the Holy Eucharist communicates to them and nourishes in them that charity towards God and humankind which is the soul of all apostolate.

"From this there flows the invitation, which I am renewing, to all laypersons, so that they may re-discover their original dignity as disciples of the Lord, may grasp more deeply the sense of their apostolic responsibility, and may make a generous contribution to the task of evangelization. . . .

"Indeed, today the Church needs mature lay people, who are true disciples and witnesses of Christ, builders of Christian communities, who transform the world according to gospel values.

"To all the lay people already active in the Church's missionary effort, I wish to address my thanks, and to encourage each one of them in his or her respective task" (World Mission Day Message, 1987).

Thus, the Holy Father calls on all laypeople to take up as a personal responsibility their proper task in evangelization. The services which they carry out in the missions and for the missions is vitally important. In this way shall we reap those fruits which the Council hoped to find in the young churches when it invited them to "devote all care to the formation of a mature Christian laity" (*Ad Gentes*, 21). And with lively satisfaction the Holy Father takes notice of these fruits, especially on the occasion of his apostolic journeys. "Ever more numerous are the laypeople who, in pastoral councils, in the exercise of various existing ministries, or in associations and movements, collaborate actively and in a qualified manner with the bishops and priests in various apostolic initiatives. This vitality of the laity in the missions is a consoling sign that the Church is developing, in the spirit willed by the Lord, of communion and collaboration" (*Osservatore Romano*, October 2, 1987).

A very special invitation to join in missionary endeavors was addressed by the Holy Father to youth, whom he called the "evangelists of the third millennium." In his act of consecration to the Virgin of Lujan (in Argentina, on April 12, 1987), the pope prayed thus: "I entrust to thee all the youth of the world, the hope of the Church and of her pastors, the evangelists of the third millennium, witnesses of the faith and love of Christ in our society and among the young" (*Osservatore Romano*, April 14, 1987).

In particular, the Holy Father encourages two forms of missionary activity which are especially lay in character: catechists, and lay volunteers.

1. Catechists

In practically none of his apostolic journeys does John Paul II fail to address words of appreciation and encouragement to those whom he has characterized as "most deserving legion," "specialized workers in mission lands," "direct witnesses to the faith," "irreplaceable," "highly deserving group of lay apostles," and so on. He has also spoken of their vocation and of their service as a "priceless work," an "irreplaceable contribution to the propagation of the faith," "a task of the highest importance," "a function of supreme necessity which the Church can never do without."

In his message for the World Mission Day in 1987, John Paul II says, speaking of catechists: "They have been, and still are, direct witnesses to the faith, at times even the first in the chronological sense to announce the gospel, thus becoming active collaborators in the process of stabilizing, developing and increasing Christian life. Their service is grafted onto the stem of evangelization, and because of this the Church cannot do without them. Once again I hope that their number and their quality may always increase, for theirs is so necessary a role that I hope they may always find the benevolence and the help they need" (*ibid.*, June 17, 1987).

At the Angelus on October 18, 1987, reechoing the theme dealt with in the Synod of Bishops then in session, and speaking of the consoling vitality of the laity in the missions, John Paul II said: "How could we fail to note in this connection, the contribution made by that deserving throng of apostolic laypeople, the catechists? It must be recognized that these make a notable contribution, and an irreplaceable one, to the propagation of the faith and of the Church. Guided by the priests, the catechists at the cost of real sacrifices teach evangelical doctrine, and organize liturgical functions and works of charity. To the catechists too I offer my gratitude and my encouragement, that they may continue generously in their most precious service" (*ibid.*, October 19, 1987).

At the beginning of his pontificate, John Paul II had written in *Catechesi Tradendae:* "But the term 'catechist' belongs above all to the catechists in mission lands" (#66). On the occasion of the Synod dedicated to the laity he decided to invite as auditors four representatives, catechists from various countries and continents, and first of all, from missionary countries.

Referring to these representatives, in the homily given on World Mission Day in 1987, he said: "You are the ones who exemplify in a large measure the missionary character of the Church. United to your bishops and priests you participate in the great, ongoing, and ever renewed work of evangelizing the world" (*Osservatore Romano*, October 19-20, 1987).

2. Lay volunteers

This is a form of lay missionary endeavor on which the Church today relies very much. "This is a valid formula which brings a notable contribution to the Church's mission, facilitating the progress of evangelization. It is a service assumed by lay Christians who undertake to offer some years of their lives to direct cooperation in the evolution of developing countries. . . . Thus, along with the work of human progress which they carry out together with others involved in social action, these men and women, as Christians, seek to provide for their brethren that fullness of religious and moral growth which can be found only when people open themselves totally to the grace of God. Inspired by faith and evangelical charity, they become witnesses of love and service for people in the totality of their corporal and spiritual being" (*ibid.*, June 17, 1987).

The Holy Father hopes that among the fruits of the recent Synod on the "vocation and ministry of the laity" the particular churches may re-discover this form of missionary cooperation, and that thus it may be possible to promote these lay vocations, which many would be glad to embrace.

Speaking of these Christian lay volunteers who, following an interior call go out to the missions and dedicate themselves to various tasks of great utility to the mission of the local church, John Paul II said: "I wish them to know that the pope is close to them, and exhorts them to be always, and above all, authentic witnesses of their faith, and concrete expressions of the exchange of charity between the churches" (*ibid.*, October 19, 1987).

7. Missionary cooperation and social betterment

Quoting the new Code of Canon Law which dedicates to missionary activity an entire part of Book III, John Paul II repeats the "obligation incumbent on all the faithful of cooperating in the evangelizing effort, each one according to his possibilities, realizing his own responsibility which flows from the intrinsically missionary nature of the Church" (cf. World Mission Day Message, 1983; cf. Canon Law 781).

The same Canon offers a juridical recognition of missionary cooperation when it indicates four basic objectives: promotion of missionary vocations; the priestly help due for mission initiatives especially for the development of the Pontifical Missionary Works; the celebration of World Mission Day; and the annual collection of funds for the missions, to be sent in to the Holy See.

"To offer such generous help is a duty, an honor, and a joy, because it means contributing to bringing the inestimable benefits of the Redemption to so many who still do not know the 'inscrutable riches of Christ' " (*ibid.*).

Today, there is emerging a new concept of cooperation, no longer understood as a one-way process, as help furnished to the younger churches by those of longer standing; but rather "as a reciprocal and fecund exchange of energy and of goods, in the atmosphere of a fraternal communion of sister churches, in transcending the dualism of 'rich churches' and 'poor churches,' as if there existed two distinct categories: the churches which 'give,' and the churches which do nothing but 'receive.' In reality there exists a true reciprocity, in so far as the poverty of a church which receives help renders richer the church which deprives itself by giving" (*Insegnamenti*, V/2, p. 1881).

Closely linked with cooperation is the task of missionary animation, understood as the task of making people aware of the problems of evangelization, and hence of the importance of their input in the sector of collaboration.

8. The Pontifical Missionary Works

"And to what structures better than to the Pontifical Missionary Works could we have recourse to activate this program of arousing awareness at the grassroots, and of organizing the network of universal charity?" (*ibid.,* VI/1, p. 1484).

John Paul II defines the Pontifical Missionary Works as "the irreplaceable instrument of missionary cooperation. . . to which always and everywhere, as *Ad Gentes* declares, must be reserved the first place, and which it is more than ever opportune to strengthen and develop in all dioceses" (*ibid.,* V/2, p. 1882).

In concluding this section dedicated to the "subjects of the mission" it is significant to cite the comment made by John Paul II in his homily on October 18, 1987, on the text from Romans, 10:14-15: "And how shall they believe if they have not heard? and how shall they hear, unless there be someone to preach?" He spoke as follows: "Let us all listen to the words of the Apostle. Listen to them, especially you missionaries, religious, and laypeople alike. Listen to them, you catechists. These questions of the Apostle Paul refer directly to you; they speak of you. The actual Bishop of Rome bears them in his heart, after the example of the Apostle.

"And echoing the apostolic words, he proclaims, together with the bishops in the Synod present here, 'the praise of your mission,' praise which we already find in the Old Testament, in the book of the prophet Isaiah: 'How beautiful on the mountains are the feet of those who bring glad tidings!' (Is 52:7)" (*Osservatore Romano*, October 19, 1987).

This praise of the mission consists in the obvious appearance of the wealth of gifts and fruits that the Holy Spirit imparts to the Church when he distributes among the faithful of all ranks special graces with which he makes them apt and ready to take upon themselves the tasks and responsibilities needed for evangelization.

John Paul II paid particular attention to the missionary role of women when he declared: "It is most desirable that this group of the laity [that is, women] should dedicate themselves either to the traditional types of activity — hospitals, schools, social services — or to direct evangelization, as in the training of family units, in dialogue with the non-believers or the non-practicing, the promotion of Catholic culture, and above all in a constant presence in the area of prayer and the liturgy" (*ibid.*, June 17, 1987).

III. DIALOGUE AS THE WAY AND METHOD OF THE MISSION

The Church was sent by Christ to reveal and to communicate the charity of God to all nations and all cultures. In order to be able to present to them the mysteries of salvation and the life that God offers to humanity, she must seek to penetrate into all human collectivities by using the same method that Christ himself used. In his Incarnation he bound himself to the socio-cultural milieu of the people in the midst of which he lived (cf. *Ad Gentes*, 10).

The Church, then, as the messenger of the Good News of Jesus Christ, strives with all her strength to proclaim the gospel. She is ever attentively questioning herself, and seeking out ways and means most appropriate for announcing the gospel to humanity, which will soon face the third millennium.

We are dealing here with a project and a methodology which bear the imprint of the divine, and which operate under the gentle yet powerful inspiration of the Holy Spirit. To this self-examination the Church replies: "Evangelization in the first place!" And to evangelize also signifies entering into an interreligious dialogue with other religions, immersing herself into the cultures of different peoples, and taking up the challenge of promoting human values.

1. Evangelization in the first place

Speaking to the bishops of Columbia during their *ad limina* visit, and quoting Puebla, John Paul II said: "The greatest service we can render to a brother or sister is evangelization, which prepares them to fulfill themselves as children of God, liberates them from injustice, and leads them to a fuller life" (*Insegnamenti*, II/2, p. 999).*

Evangelization, therefore, must remain the first way and the principal duty of the mission. It should not let itself be distracted by other aims, even noble ones, as John Paul II recently insisted, speaking to the bishops of Tanzania during their *ad limina* visit: "The witness of an exemplary Christian life is already an act of evangelization. But I hasten to add that the testimony of a Christian life by means of example is not enough, in itself. It must be preceded and accompanied by the proclamation of the Good News of salvation in Christ, which stands at the center of all the evangelizing action of the Church. And both of these essential elements must be sustained by prayer and sacrifice" (*Osservatore Romano*, December 5, 1987).

It is appropriate here to repeat the words of John Paul II already quoted above: "Either the Church is a missionary Church or it is not even evangelical any longer."

2. Interreligious dialogue

In the thinking of John Paul II dialogue is for the Church, in a certain sense, a means, and especially a mode of carrying out her action in the world of today. For her, "dialogue is absolutely necessary, because otherwise evangelization would remain a dead letter" (*Insegnamenti*, VI/1, p. 148).

The meeting at Assisi on October 27, 1986, was for John Paul II an occasion for demonstrating concretely what the Catholic Church understands by dialogue with members of other religions. Speaking to the Roman Curia on December 22, 1986, the pope brought out the role of the Church as a sign and instrument of

---

*   See also the discourse to the Latin American Bishops Conference in Santo Domingo in 1984: "Evangelization must uplift humanity, giving them above all faith, salvation in Christ, the means and the instruction to obtain these. For truly poor are those who lack material necessities, but even poorer are those who are ignorant of the path that God points out to them, who have not received the grace of divine filiation, who do not know the moral path which leads to the happy eternal destiny to which God calls us" (Osservatore Romano, October 14, 1984).

unity for the entire human race. He declared: "The Assisi meeting can thus be considered as a visible illustration and an object lesson, a catechesis intelligible to all, about what is presupposed and signified by our ecumenical duty and the obligation to undertake interreligious dialogue recommended and promoted by Vatican II.

"It presented the Catholic Church as stretching out her hands to our Christian brethren; and these all together joined hands with brethren of other religions, so that day in Assisi was, as it were, a visible expression of these affirmations of Vatican II. In this way, and through this meeting we succeeded by God's grace in putting into practice, with no shadow of confusion or syncretism, this conviction of ours, taught us by the Council, concerning the unity in principle and the finality of the human family, and about the meaning and the value of non-Christian religions" (*Osservatore Romano*, December 22, 1986).

Interreligious dialogue as a "way" of evangelization was courageously affirmed by John Paul II when he said that "the Catholic Church at every level is committed to frank ecumenical dialogue without facile optimism, but also without distrust and without hesitation or delays" (cf. *Reconciliatio et Paenitentia*, 25).

We thus find in the language of John Paul II the word "frank" which means that dialogue, to be constructive, must be based on the clarity of its premises, and on its fidelity and conformity to the faith transmitted and defined in the light of the constant tradition of the magisterium.

Frankness also means rejecting any shadow of confusion or syncretism. Wherefore, dialogue cannot mean renouncing in any way the call and the missionary mandate which the Church has been given to illuminate the whole world with the gospel message, and to bring together in a single spirit the whole of humanity. True dialogue, then, must be compatible both with the "mission" and with "conversion": with the mission in the sense that dialogue, in so far as it is a "way" for evangelization, permits the Christian to offer to his interlocutor the possibility of experiencing in an existential manner the values of the gospel; with "conversion" in the sense that every missionary proclamation is aimed at conversion. "Only in this way will the non-Christians, whose hearts the Holy Spirit will open, believe, will freely turn to the Lord, and sincerely adhere to Him" (*Ad Gentes*, 13).

In this perspective, commenting on the First Letter of St. Peter, John Paul II indicated a passage found there as "the golden rule governing the relationships between Christians and their fellow citizens of different faiths: 'Adore the Lord Christ in your hearts always ready to satisfy everyone with a reason for that hope which is in you, but with modesty, having a good conscience' (1 P 3:15)" (to Christians at Ankara, November 29, 1979).

In strict consonance between dialogue and mission, on the occasion of his twenty-ninth apostolic visit, to the churches of India, John Paul II spoke thus to the Indian bishops gathered at New Delhi: "Interreligious dialogue is an important part of the bishops' apostolic ministry. Because of this they should do all they can to promote such dialogue, conformably to the Church's obligation; a dialogue made up of courteous respect, of meekness and good faith, from which there should be excluded all rivalry and polemics. A dialogue that springs from faith, and is carried on with humble affection."

Still, after these preliminary words, he went on to declare: "As the ministers of the gospel here in India yours is the duty to give witness to your convictions based on faith, and to offer the gospel of love and peace in Christ, and his spirit of service to the consideration of those who freely desire to reflect thereupon. In this interreligious dialogue which by its very nature implies collaboration, the supreme norms are charity and truth" (*Osservatore Romano*, February 3, 1986).

In that same journey, meeting at Madras with members of non-Christian religions, John Paul II said: "The Church teaches that every human being has a right to religious liberty. This liberty means that everyone must be free from coercion, by individuals or by social groups, or by any other human power, so that nobody may be forced to act against his own convictions. In the preamble to its Constitution India guarantees to all citizens. . . liberty of religion. The religious leaders should uphold and defend that precious principle which also includes the right to profess, to practice, and to propagate religion" (*ibid.*, February 6, 1986).

Again, as a sign of frankness and charity joined to faithfulness to the mission, John Paul II, at the close of his journey to Africa, in 1985, desired to meet at Casablanca, Morocco, with a group of young Muslims; and speaking to them he did not fail to bear witness to that faith and that hope he bears within him as one who believes in Christ, and as the supreme Pastor of the Catholic Church. "As for myself, in the Catholic Church I occupy the position of the Successor of Peter, the Apostle, whom Jesus chose to confirm his brethren in the faith. After all the other popes who without interruption throughout history have succeeded each other I today am the Bishop of Rome, called to be, among my brethren in the world, a witness to the faith and a pledge of the unity of all the members of the Church.

"Hence, it is as a believer that I come to you today. It is in all simplicity that I should like to bear witness here to what I believe in, what I desire for the happiness of my fellow human beings, and what by experience I believe is useful for all: Believe in God!" (*ibid.*, August 21, 1985).

In what we might call this "missionary dialogue" the Church speaks to people of their transcendent destiny; reasons with them about justice, liberty, truth, progress, concord, peace, civilization. The secret of these realities the Church knows, because Christ has revealed them to her; she also knows that she cannot keep to herself this revelation, but must necessarily communicate it to all humanity, so that all peoples may enter into contact with Christ the Savior.

"Every person without any exception whatever has been redeemed by Christ; and because with every human person, without any exception whatever, Christ is in a way united, even when one is unaware of this, Christ, who died and was raised up for all, provides each and every person with the light and the strength to measure up to that supreme calling" (*Redemptor Hominis*, 14).

For the Church, dialogue does not arise from tactical opportunism, but solely from the fact that hers is a mission of love, making her the leaven and the soul of society. . . to renew it in Christ and make it God's family (cf. *Lumen Gentium*, 9).

Like Christ, so too his disciples, intimately filled with the Spirit, "must know the people in the midst of whom they live, and bring their relationships with them to a sincere and comprehensive dialogue, demonstrating all the richness that God in His generosity has given to peoples, and at the same time striving to illuminate these riches with the light of the Gospel, and to liberate them and connect them to the rule of God our Savior" (*Ad Gentes*, 11).

3. Evangelization of different cultures

This problem too, so closely connected with the evangelization of peoples, is amply treated in the magisterium of John Paul II.

Paul VI clearly brought out how urgent this problem is for the missionary Church, when he declared that "the rupture between the Gospel and culture is no doubt the drama of our epoch" (*Evangelii Nuntiandi*, 20). With equal vigor John Paul II has said that "the division between faith and culture is more than a small impediment to evangelization" (*Sapientia Christiana*, foreword).

The missionary Church cannot, therefore, play down the importance of this problem, and must strive with all the strength needed to evangelize the various cultures, "not in a merely 'decorative' way, by applying a thin veneer, but in a vital way, in depth, and right down to their very roots" (*Evangelii Nuntiandi*, 20).

All this is so, as John Paul II took care to point out, because the word "inculturation" although newly coined, "expresses very well one factor of the great mystery of the Incarnation" (*Catechesi Tradendae*, 53).

The pontiff himself seems to offer us a definition of this problem when in his encyclical *Slavorum Apostoli* he writes: "The work of evangelization which they [Cyril and Methodius] carried out, as pioneers in the territory inhabited by the Slav people, contains both a model of what today is called 'inculturation' — the incarnation of the Gospel in native cultures — and also the introduction of these cultures into the life of the Church" (*Slavorum Apostoli*, 21).

Once we affirm the validity and the importance of inculturation, we need to indicate also the main norms which should govern its application. Since this process closely borders on the truth of faith, we must proceed with great prudence, so that (and these are also the words of John Paul II) "the cross of Christ may not be made vain" (*Catechesi Tradendae*, 53).

In his apostolic exhortation *Familiaris Consortio* (November 22, 1981), John Paul seems to indicate two major features needed for a correct "inculturation," namely "compatibility with the Gospel of the various cultures to be addressed, and communion with the universal Church" (#10).

Compatibility with the gospel. There cannot be any inculturation unless the integrity of evangelical truth is safeguarded. The power of the gospel is a transforming and regenerating one; it should penetrate culture, "rectifying" those out-of-date elements (not a few in number) which exist in them, "helping them to go beyond the defective or even inhuman features found in them" (*Catechesi Tradendae*, 53).

Communion with the universal Church. When John Paul II went "as a pilgrim to the sanctuary of the People of God" in India and spoke to the bishops gathered in New Delhi, he had the opportunity to take up this major theme of inculturation. "In this task of insuring a genuine and faithful adaptation" he mentioned, among other things: "The bishops have a specific responsibility, one exercised in close collaboration with the Holy See, and in communion with the entire Church. This implies discernment, which in its turn calls for prayer, study, and consultation — a discernment upheld by the pastoral charism."

Continuing his allocution, he called the bishops' attention especially to the question of "liturgical inculturation," and added: "Here, we need more reflection and study. Here it is also important that doctrinal verification and pastoral preparation of the faithful should always precede the application of liturgical norms" (*Osservatore Romano*, February 3, 1986).

Let us conclude this reflection on the characteristics of a proper inculturation by recalling a precious passage of John Paul II: "The mission is never destruction; instead it is a taking up and fresh building, even if in practice there has not always been full correspondence with this high ideal" (*Redemptor Hominis*, 12).

Incarnation in a culture should not, therefore, mean confusion with the culture, by the same principle in virtue of which Christ, as the Word of God, was not "contaminated" by human nature, but rather "assumed" it in order to redeem it (cf. *Ad Gentes*, 3:15).

The gospel should transcend all cultures; it should animate them and impregnate them by a process which will at the same time be an assumption, a purification, a transfiguration, without ever permitting that it should become impoverished, without abdicating or attenuating its message, without any compromise in the "good deposit of faith," without stooping to "concessions in matters of faith or morals" (*Catechesi Tradendae*, 53).

4. Evangelization and human advancement

Evangelization, as an authentic proclamation of the mystery of the redeeming Christ, necessarily involves as well a renewal of human beings and of society, its progress and liberation from various evils, the development and growth of social justice and respect for the dignity and the rights of persons. The missionary Church, therefore, knows that by building up the kingdom of God it also renders service to the world. Evangelization, consequently, is bound in a deep and manifold manner to the task of human development.

However, according to *Gaudium et Spes,* "we must carefully distinguish this earthly process from the growth of the kingdom of Christ" (#39). And with *Evangelii Nuntiandi* we must remember that "the Church connects, but never identifies, human liberation and salvation in Jesus Christ" (#35).

Hence, the service and the progress of humanity remain "ways" or methods of evangelization, springing from the conviction that the gospel is an authentic message of liberation.

John Paul II has repeatedly intervened to clarify both the points where evangelization and human progress meet, and those where they differ.

In his address at the inauguration of the third Conference of the Latin American Episcopate at Puebla, he said: "The truth which we owe to humanity is above all a truth concerning humanity itself. As witnesses of Jesus Christ we are heralds, mouthpieces, servants of that truth which we cannot reduce to the principles of a philosophical system, or to mere political activity. We cannot forget it, or betray it" (*Insegnamenti*, II, p. 219-20).

Speaking to the bishops of the Republic of Santo Domingo during his Latin American journey (January 25, 1979), John Paul II said: "The proclamation of the gospel cannot be dissociated from human advancement; but for the Church the former cannot be identified with, nor limit itself, as some pretend, to the latter. This would be to shut humanity out of the infinite space which God has opened before it, and to falsify the deepest and most complete meaning of evangelization, which is above all the proclaiming of the Good News of Christ our Savior" (*ibid.,* 130).

In the same address, however, John Paul II affirmed: "But do not be satisfied with bringing about this more human world; bring about a world that is explicitly more divine, more according to God, strong in faith, and in which the Church may inspire the moral, religious, and social progress of humanity. Do not lose sight of the vertical dimension of evangelization. This has the power to liberate humanity because it is the revelation of love; the love of the Father for human beings, for each and every human person, a love revealed in Christ Jesus" (*ibid.*).*

During his thirtieth apostolic journey, John Paul II, speaking to the Latin American Bishops Conference took the occasion to come back on these notions when he said: "If we are faithful to the Spirit, to the Word, and to the Church of Jesus Christ we shall also be faithful to humanity, in whose service, especially that of the poorest and most needy, we have been sent as messengers of salvation" (cf. *Osservatore Romano*, April 7, 1986).

Since evangelization is a work of salvation, such salvation must be integral salvation for the entire human person. For this reason in the teaching of John Paul II we find great care to maintain clearly and firmly the unity and at the same time the distinction between evangelization and human advancement: the unity, because evangelization seeks the total good of humanity; the distinction, because these two undertakings are included, but under different titles, in her mission.

CONCLUSION

We have paused to read that great lesson of evangelization offered to us in John Paul II's enlightened teaching.

From this teaching, so ample in quantity and so deep in quality, there shines forth, in all its splendor, the commitment and the faithfulness to continue the mission entrusted by Christ to his Church: "Go, teach all nations," and in particular to Peter and to his successors the commission to "confirm thy brethren" (Mt 28:19; Lk 22:32).

This mission appears, ever more and more, as the proclamation of the mystery of trinitarian love; the mystery which in

---

* *See also the address to the Latin American Bishops Conference in Santo Domingo in 1984 (*Osservatore Romano, *October 14, 1984).*

Christ, the Redeemer of the world, has penetrated, in a unique and unrepeatable manner, into the mystery of humanity.

Besides repeating this proclamation, the mission must see to it that each individual person may, in turn, enter into Christ with his whole self, to the point of appropriating to himself and of assimilating all the realities of the Incarnation and the Redemption, to find once again his original vocation as a child of God, sanctified by the gift of the Spirit.

Since Christ is the New Person who "reveals fully to mankind what it really is" (*Gaudium et Spes*, 22) only in him can every human creature find the greatness, the dignity, and the value which properly belong to its humanity.

The human person is also the first highway that the Church must traverse in the accomplishment of her mission; the human person is the first and fundamental way of the Church (cf. *Redemptor Hominis*, 14).

In this teaching we have sought to pinpoint those solid contents and those necessary clarifications, capable of motivating and sustaining adequately the missionary commitment of every one of the faithful and of every Christian community, in the hope that through every one of the Church's members, participation in her universal evangelizing mission may indeed become a basic law of life.

All this will be possible thanks to the guidance and the protection of Mary, Queen of the missions, and Star of evangelization. Looking upon her and imitating her who goes before us and accompanies us in our pilgrimage of faith, as the pontiff so felicitously reminds us, it will be easier to understand and to put into action in all its fullness the deepest meaning of the mission.

By having recourse to her intercession it will also be possible to rejuvenate in each one concern for evangelization, and responsibility for the proclamation of the gospel.

> *Josef Cardinal Tomko*
> *Prefect of the Congregation*
> *for the Evangelization of*
> *Peoples*

(Translated from Italian by Richard Arnandez, FSC)

THE FAMILY IN THE MAGISTERIUM OF JOHN PAUL II

Bishop Darió Castrillón

The family surely enjoys high priority among the pastoral concerns of our Holy Father, Pope John Paul II. We are scarcely surprised, then, to discover an abundance of material on this subject in his magisterial pronouncements.

I shall confine my considerations here to certain reflections on the apostolic exhortation, *Familiaris Consortio*, and some passages from certain papal pronouncements made in Latin America.

The Holy Father consistently holds before our eyes an image of the human being as seen in the light of Christ. He has rehabilitated the authentic image of the human being.

The pope's point of departure, the key to an understanding of the human being, is Christ.

> So we must profess Christ before history and the world, displaying the same deeply felt and deeply lived conviction that Peter did in his profession: "You are the Messiah. . .the Son of the living God" (Mt 16:16). (Pope John Paul II, "Opening Address at the Puebla Conference," I, I, 3, in *Puebla and Beyond*, ed. John Eagleson and Philip Scharper [Maryknoll, N.Y.: Orbis Books, 1979], 59)

It is in this light, then, that we must consider the human being in marriage and in the family.

We can say of the family what the Holy Father has said of the human being. "Perhaps one of the most glaring weaknesses of present-day civilization lies in an inadequate view of the human being. Undoubtedly our age is the age. . .when human values have been trodden underfoot as never before" (*ibid.*, I, I, 9, 63).

Among the values most severely threatened is the family, and the pope takes up its defense forthrightly and consistently.

Knowing that marriage and the family constitute one of the most precious of human values, the Church wishes to speak and offer her help to those who are already aware of the value of marriage and the family and seek to live it faithfully, to those who are uncertain and anxious and searching for the truth, and to those who are unjustly impeded from living freely their family lives. Supporting the first, illuminating the second and assisting the others, the Church offers her services to every person who wonders about the destiny of marriage and the family. (*Familiaris Consortio*, 1)

I. HISTORICAL DIMENSION

The Holy Father examines the family in all the fullness of its value and historical being, subject as it is to the dynamism and vicissitudes of history.

Having adopted this viewpoint, the sovereign pontiff regards the potential and the difficulties of the family at the present moment as far from unimportant.

It is the families involved in the present conditions of the world that are called to accept and live the plan of God that pertains to them. Moreover, the call and demands of the Spirit resound in the very events of history, and so the Church can also be guided to a more profound understanding of the inexhaustible mystery of marriage and the family by the circumstances, the questions and the anxieties and hopes of the young people, married couples and parents of today. (*Ibid.*, 4)

II. THE FAMILY IN ITS NATURAL BEING

In the Christian humanism so tirelessly preached by Pope John Paul II, the natural being of the family cannot be rendered independent of the will of the Creator.

The family must go back to the "beginning" of God's creative act, if it is to attain self-knowledge and self-realization in accordance with the inner truth not only of what it is but also of what it does in history. And since in God's plan it has been established as an "intimate community of life and love," the family has the mission to become more and more what it is, that is to say, a community of life and love. . . . Looking at it in such a way as to reach its very roots, we must say that the essence and role of the family are in the final analysis specified by love. (*Ibid.,* 17)

In the natural being of the family, three key factors come together: *love*, which is the essence of the family; *life*, which is the fruit and sign of love; and *community*, in which this fertile love finds its highest realization.

1. Love

In creating us to the divine image and likeness, God gives man and woman the vocation, the capacity, and the responsibility of love and communion (*ibid.,* 11).

In marriage, love fully responds to the human being's twin dimensions of spirit and matter. "As an incarnate spirit, that is a soul which expresses itself in a body and a body informed by an immortal spirit, man is called to love in his unified totality" (*ibid.*). Here we have a compendium of all of the richness of John Paul's magisterium on human sexuality. *Familiaris Consortio* summarizes his teaching as follows.

Love includes the human body, and the body is made a sharer in spiritual love. . . .
Consequently, sexuality, by means of which man and woman give themselves to one another through the acts which are proper and exclusive to spouses, is by no means something purely biological, but concerns the innermost being of the human person as such. It is realized in a truly human way only if it is an integral part of the love by which a man and a woman commit themselves totally to one another until death. (*Ibid.*)

In a world fallen victim to hatred, deceived by false love, and frustrated by perversions of love, the family is the archetype of love.

The institution of marriage is not an undue interference by society or authority, nor the extrinsic imposition of a form. Rather it is an interior requirement of the covenant of conjugal love which is publicly affirmed as unique and exclusive, in order to live in complete fidelity to the plan of God, the Creator (*ibid.*).

2. Life

The Holy Father does not hesitate to assert that "the fundamental task of the family is to serve life, to actualize in history the original blessing of the Creator—that of transmitting by procreation the divine image from person to person" (*ibid., 28*).

We must confess that we are witnessing a universal depreciation of the value of life today. A philosophy of pleasure has destroyed the relationship between sex and life, bestowing an absolute primacy on the former and divorcing it from the normal term of its relation, or life. This attitude has actually led to the legal recognition of homosexual unions.

Again, violence is sovereign in our world, and in our days has attained the widest variety of expression, from abortion, war, and terrorism, to euthanasia.

In the face of this situation, the pope declares that the great task of renewing society will be based on a return to an understanding of the ultimate meaning of life and its basic values (*ibid., 8*). Precisely because conjugal love is a singular participation in the mystery of the very life and love of God, the Church knows that it has received the special mission of safeguarding the exalted dignity of marriage and the most grave responsibility of the transmission of human life (cf. *ibid., 28*).

> The Church firmly believes that this human life, frail and weak as it is, is ever the splendid gift of the God of goodness. In the face of the pessimism and selfishness that becloud our world, the Church comes forward in favor of life, and is able to discover, in every human life, the splendor of that "Yes," that "Amen," that is Christ himself. To the "no" that invades and afflicts our world, the Church opposes this living "Yes," thereby defending

the human being and the world from all who assault and demean life. (*Ibid.,* 30)

3. Community

Pope John Paul II takes up the teaching of Vatican Council II, placing the family at the base of all community development.

"The creator of the world has established the conjugal society as the origin and foundation of human society" (*ibid.,* 42). The family is therefore the "first, vital cell of society."

While the deterioration of family values has led more than a few to fail to recognize the basic role of marriage and the family in society, the pope reasserts the irreplaceable value of the family institution.

> The family has vital, organic links with society, as it constitutes the latter's foundation and ongoing nourishment by way of its function of service to life. After all, citizens are born in families, and it is in the family that they find the first school of the social virtues that are the animating principle of the existence and development of society itself. (*Ibid.*)

The fostering of authentic and mature communion between persons within the family is the first and irreplaceable school of social life, and example and stimulus for the broader community relationships marked by respect, justice, dialogue and love (*ibid.,* 43).

III. THE FAMILY IN ITS ECCLESIAL BEING

The reality and potential of the life of faith in the Christian family motivated the Second Vatican Council to refer to the family as the "domestic Church."

Pastoral experience teaches us that faith is transmitted, taught, nourished, and lived in the nucleus of the family.

Since the first evangelization, in countries suffering from a notable shortage of clergy, the family has been the pillar and bulwark of faith. This is the case in Latin America, where family values are still strong.

> Christian marriage and the Christian family build up the Church: for in the family the human person is not only brought into being and progressively introduced by means of education into the human community, but by means of the rebirth of baptism and education in the faith the child is also introduced into God's family, which is the Church. . . .
>
> Christian marriage. . .constitutes the natural setting in which the human person is introduced into the great family of the Church. (*Ibid.,* 15)

The sanctifying potential of the family springs from the Sacrament of Marriage.

> By virtue of the sacramentality of their marriage, spouses are bound to one another in the most profoundly indissoluble manner. Their belonging to each other is the real representation, by means of the sacramental sign, of the very relationship of Christ with the Church.
>
> Spouses are therefore the permanent reminder to the Church of what happened on the Cross; they are for one another and for the children witnesses to the salvation in which the sacrament makes them sharers. (*Ibid.,* 13)

Through their union with God in the sacrament of marriage, spouses become a reflection of that love of God that is "not solitude, but family." They are transformed into an authentic human archetype of love. Thus, in John Paul II's wonderful expression, the family is a revelation of love.

> The family has the mission to guard, reveal and communicate love, and this is a living reflection of and a real sharing in God's love for humanity and the love of Christ the Lord for the Church His bride. (*Ibid.,* 17)

IV. MISSION OF THE FAMILY TODAY

From its natural being and its ecclesial being, the family's mission in the Church and the world arises.

The Holy Father lists the four general tasks of the family that were set in relief by the Synod on the family. Three of these emanate from the natural being of the family, the fourth from its ecclesial being.

1. Formation of a community of persons
2. Service to life
3. Sharing in the development of society
4. Sharing in the life and mission of the Church

I have already alluded to the first three tasks in speaking of the natural being of the family. Thus I shall add only one reflection on the third, and dwell a bit longer on the fourth.

The Latin American episcopate has maintained a particular interest in the subject of the family, the development of society, and development in general. The General Conferences of Medellín and Puebla have dealt with the family as a molder of persons and promoter of development.

Pope John Paul states that, as the bishops recalled at the Synod, the family constitutes the natural place, and most effective tool, of the humanization and personalization of society. It cooperates in an original, profound manner in the construction of the world, making it possible to lead a genuinely human life, especially by safeguarding and transmitting virtues and values (cf. *ibid.*, 43).

The commitment of the family to development is very important in Latin America, by virtue of the social significance attached to the family on our continent. Pope John Paul II reminded the bishops gathered at Puebla of the teaching of the bishops in the Medellín Conference, who "saw in your great family feeling a primordial trait of your Latin American culture" ("Homily in Puebla," 2, in *Puebla and Beyond*, 78).

> Families. . .either singly or in association, can and should devote themselves to manifold social service activities, especially in favor of the poor, or at any rate for the benefit of all people and situations that cannot be reached by the public authorities' welfare organization. . . .
> The social role of families is called upon to find expression

also in the form of *political intervention*: families should be the first to take steps to see that the laws and institutions of the State not only do not offend but support and positively defend the rights and duties of the family. (*Familiaris Consortio*, 44)

V. SHARING IN THE LIFE AND MISSION OF THE CHURCH

Quoting Pope Paul VI, John Paul II declared in Santo Domingo that the Church exists in order to evangelize. "Evangelization constitutes its felicity, and its deepest calling and identity." The family should be fully committed to this calling and identity of the Church.

> Among the basic duties of the Christian family is its ecclesial charge and task. The family should be at the service of the building of the Reign of God in history, through participation in the life and mission of the Church. (*Ibid.*, 49)

This has been the ongoing task of the family in Latin America. Despite the crises that have shaken the institution of the family, in Latin America as much as anywhere, especially in our large cities and their outskirts, the family continues to be the vessel and vehicle of Christian values. With the shortage of priests and the remoteness of existing parishes, the family has sometimes been the sole educator in the faith, and has carried out its task with dedication and effectiveness. As Pope Paul VI said in *Evangelii Nuntiandi*, "the family, like the Church, ought to be a place where the Gospel is transmitted and from which the Gospel radiates" (#71).

John Paul II recalls that the Synod, taking up the call he issued at Puebla, has repeated that future evangelization depends in large part on the "domestic Church." And he adds:

> The ministry of evangelization carried out by Christian parents is original and irreplaceable. It assumes the characteristics typical of family life itself, which should be

interwoven with love, simplicity, practicality and daily witness. (*Familiaris Consortio*, 53)

With the celebration of the fifth centenary of the coming of the cross and the gospel to America, the Holy Father has invited us to undertake a new evangelization—new in its fervor, new in its methods, and new in its expressions. Taking our cue from the pope, we find the most reliable support for this new kind of evangelization in the family.

The institution of the family is still strong in Latin America, as we have already observed. Still, we are the shepherds of this continent, and thus we continue to be confronted with the challenge of the Christian consolidation of our families. The Holy Father has told us in Santo Domingo: "Let there not be so many wrongly constituted, broken, divided, and inadequately supported families!" The pope's warning is an exhortation of universal cogency and validity. The task is evangelization, and its hope is the family.

CONCLUSION

Pope John Paul II has shown himself a visionary when it comes to the reality of the family in our world today. And he has favored the Church with a rich store of magisterial material in its regard. Both shepherds and their flock will do well to avail themselves of his pronouncements in order to plumb the depths of God's marvelous project, the family.

Might the loneliness, the lack of love, the spirit of aggression, and the anguish that afflict today's human being not be partly the result of a deterioration of the genuine sense of family, and a lack of understanding of the crisis that is currently assaulting this basic institution?

This question throbs in our pastoral hearts. Pope John Paul has shown us how to respond.

Bishop Darió Castrillón
President of the Latin
American Bishops Conference

(Translated from Spanish by Robert R. Barr)

THE TRUTH OF THE HUMAN
BEING IN CHRIST

Alfonso Cardinal López Trujillo

INTRODUCTION

This theme clearly belongs to the core of the official teaching and pastoral activity of our Holy Father, Pope John Paul II. We must surely say that, among the broad lines initiated by Vatican Council II, which is so warmly embraced by the pope as a source of inspiration and renewal, the wealth of the Christian anthropology condensed in the great chapters of the pastoral constitution *Gaudium et Spes*, in whose composition he played an active part, finds its place at the very heart of his fruitful magisterium.

John Paul has wished before all else to be a teacher of the faith. Accordingly, in the discharge of his ministry as successor of Peter he has proclaimed the gospel of Christ to the ends of the earth. His teaching is so rich and nuanced, and the documents issuing from his pen and heart in the accomplishment of his pastoral mission so many, that it becomes difficult to keep abreast of the abundance of material. I regard it as a high honor to be asked to make a contribution to the present volume. My assignment is to compose a résumé of our Holy Father's magisterial pronouncements in the area of the family, with special attention to its repercussions and application in Latin America, in his principal interventions — in his encyclicals, at the Puebla Conference (which of course will have a very particular importance), and in his discourses and homilies on the occasion of his pastoral visits to Latin America.

It is most significant that the Holy Father's first encyclical, *Redemptor Hominis*, which appeared at the beginning of his pontificate (March 4, 1979), takes such a strikingly anthropological approach, in the indispensable framework of the truth about the human being drawn from Revelation. Various of the subjects broached by him in his opening address at the Third General Conference of the Latin American Episcopate, celebrated in

Puebla, Mexico, are taken up and broadened in that encyclical.

ELEMENTS OF THIS TRUTH

Let us briefly recall some of the main elements of this material.

The truth concerning what the human being is in God's plan is revealed to us in Christ.

> He who is the "image of the invisible God" (Col 1:15), is himself the perfect man who has restored in the children of Adam that likeness to God which had been disfigured ever since the first sin. Human nature, by the very fact that it was assumed, not absorbed, in him, has been raised in us also to a dignity beyond compare. (*Redemptor Hominis*, 8; citing *Gaudium et Spes*, 22)

John Paul's point of departure is the foursquare vision of Vatican Council II: "The truth is that only in the mystery of the Incarnate Word does the mystery of man take on light" (*ibid.*). The assertion is a basic one, and has its explanation in the fact that "Christ, the Redeemer of the world, is the one who penetrated in a unique, unrepeatable way into the mystery of man and entered his 'heart'" (*ibid.*). Christian anthropology rests on a contemplation of the human being in Christ and from the standpoint of Christ. Its categories are not the achievements of human ingenuity, but of a contemplation of the One who is the image of the Father and hence the perfect archetype of the human being.

The sole key to the discovery of the mystery of the human being and of what constitutes the proper fulfillment of that being, to the extent that such a mystery can be penetrated, is an approach to Christ. The pope says:

> The man who wishes to understand himself thoroughly. . .must, so to speak, enter into [Christ] with all his own self, he must "appropriate" and assimilate the whole of the reality of the Incarnation and Redemption in order to find himself. . . . This amazement, which is also a convic-

tion and a certitude—at its deepest root it is the certainty of faith, but in a hidden and mysterious way it vivifies every aspect of authentic humanism—is closely connected with Christ. (*Redemptor Hominis*, 10)

The great truth about the human being (and this is a constant teaching of the pontifical magisterium) is that the human being is the image of God. This is the human being's historical concretion and deepest reality.

Accordingly, what is in question here is man in all his truth, in his full magnitude. We are not dealing with the "abstract" man, but the real, "concrete," "historical" man. We are dealing with "each" man, for each one is included in the mystery of the Redemption and with each one Christ has united himself for ever through this mystery. Every man. . .on account of the mystery of the Redemption is entrusted to the solicitude of the Church. Her solicitude is about the whole man and is focussed on him in an altogether special manner. The object of her care is man in his unique unrepeatable human reality, which keeps intact the image and likeness of God himself. The Council points out this very fact when, speaking of that likeness, it recalls that "man is the only creature on earth that God willed for itself." (*Redemptor Hominis*, 13; citing, *sub fine*, *Gaudium et Spes*, 24)

The truth about the human being has its explanation, then, and deepest foundation, in Christ. Pope Paul VI's exquisite portrait comes spontaneously to mind.

The Church of the Council. . .has been deeply concerned with man as he presents himself in his reality today: living man. . . . Every phenomenal man. . .clad in the vesture of his innumerable presentations. . .tragic man, in his own dramas, the superman of yesterday and today—frail and false, then, selfish and fierce—versatile man, rigid man. . .man as he is, thinking, loving, toiling. . . . The religion of God become man has collided with the religion—for this is what it is—of man become God. (Paul VI, Closing Address of Vatican Council II, 8)
Thus the Catholic religion and human life reaffirm their

covenant, their convergence in one human reality: the Catholic religion is for humanity. It is life, in virtue of the accurate, and sublime, interpretation that our religion gives of man. . .and it gives that interpretation precisely by virtue of its science of God: in order to know the human being, the genuine human being, one must know God. . . . It is life because it describes his nature and his destiny, and bestows upon him his authentic meaning. (*Ibid.,* 15)

Pope John Paul II teaches that the Church is the guardian of this truth concerning the human being. It is this truth, and not the "truth" that each one may construct for himself or herself, that matters.

Nobody, therefore, can make of theology as it were a simple collection of his own personal ideas, but everybody must be aware of being in close union with the mission of teaching truth for which the Church is responsible. (*Redemptor Hominis*, 19)

He had emphasized this truth about the human being before the publication of *Redemptor Hominis* — a little more than a month before — in his opening address at the Puebla Conference. We must recall that this celebrated discourse stood on the tripod, as it were, of a threefold truth: the truth about Christ, the truth about the Church, and the truth about the human being. Concerning the last of these truths, the Holy Father recalls: "The Church has the right and the duty to proclaim the truth about the human being that it received from its teacher, Jesus Christ." This truth has been revealed to it "by him who knew 'what was in man's heart' (Jn 2:25)." And this proclamation is "the best service to human beings" that can be rendered ("Opening Address at the Puebla Conference," I, I, 9, in *Puebla and Beyond*, ed. John Eagleson and Philip Scharper [Maryknoll, N.Y.: Orbis Books, 1979], 64).

Thanks to the Gospel, the Church possesses the truth about the human being. It is found in an anthropology that the Church never ceases to explore more deeply and to share. The primordial assertion of this anthropology is that the human being is the image of God. . . . This is the sense intended by St. Irenaeus when he wrote: "The glory of the human being is God; but the receptacle of all God's activity, wisdom, and power is the human being." (*Ibid.,* 63; citing St. Irenaeus, *Adversus Haereses*, III, 20, 2-3)

The Holy Father repeats the central thought of his first Christmas Message: "Christmas is the feast of the human being. . . . The human being is single, unique, and unrepeatable, someone thought of and chosen from eternity, someone called and identified by name" (Opening Address at Puebla, I, I, 9, 63-64).

This core conception of Christian anthropology is presented as the just, coherent, integral and not pared down or mutilated, conception of the human being, as over against another, "inadequate view of the human being" proclaimed in a civilization such as ours today.

> Undoubtedly our age is the age that has written and spoken the most about the human being. . . . But paradoxically it is also the age of people's deepest anxieties about their identity and destiny; it is the age when human beings have been debased to previously unsuspected levels, when human values have been trodden underfoot as never before. (*Ibid.,* 63)

Underlying this truth concerning the human being as the image of God are the following premises.

1. *The human being is not a god, or a superman, but God's creature*

The human being is created. The human being has issued from the very hands of God – lovingly molded, formed with the solicitude and tenderness of a potter bending over a surpassingly beautiful piece of art. The human being received life at the primordial wafting of spirit, and lives by the breath of life that constitutes him or her a living person. The human being lives in virtue of the breath of God. This is the beautiful picture presented in Genesis, its poetic images charged with vitality in order to transmit its basic message (cf. Gn 2:7, 1:26, 27).

The "Let us make man" is a divine decision, in which God, as it were, wills to become involved in creation in an even more intimate and intense way. Creation is the work of God alone. "To our image and likeness," we read. The Hebrew term is *selem* (image), and it indicates a correspondence between something created and the original model. The human being has been created according to the form, the archetype, the image, of God.

Human beings are not self-explanatory. They do not explain their own mystery. They are not self-sufficient. The human being is a creature, caught up in a dialogue of life with God. Men and women are loved by God with a creative love that constitutes the font of their outstanding dignity, a dignity that has been plumbed by New Testament revelation and enhanced with an enriched theology of the image of God.

2. To be the divine image is a reality and a calling

Human beings *are* because they have been *given* all that they have. Whatever they possess is a gift. This is what is implied in the concept of creation. The goodness, the reality of their being is the fruit of the divine *bará*, the fruit of God's creation. It is God, in the Thomistic conception, who infuses all things with goodness. The created is good, but the human being is especially good.

The human being ought to be the image of God in response to God's call to humanity — God's plan for humanity in general and for each human being in particular. At stake is freedom and the meaning of freedom. This is our task: to become like unto God. And it is a calling — a calling to a dynamic process of approach to that perfect image of the Father that is Christ.

The positive use of freedom — freedom in its deepest sense — is indicated by John Paul II in *Redemptor Hominis* precisely in direct conjunction with the task of being the image of God. The accomplishment of our task will "produce a mature humanity in each one of us. Mature humanity means full use of the gift of freedom received from the Creator when he called to existence the man made 'in his image, after his likeness' " (*Redemptor Hominis*, 21).

Freedom is a great gift only when we know how to use it consciously for everything that is our true good. Christ teaches us that the best use of freedom is charity (*ibid.*).

127

3. To be the image of God supposes a responsibility toward nature and creation

Fashioned in the image and likeness of God, the human being is commissioned as God's representative in the complex whole of creation. The human being is, as it were, God's ambassador, or grand vizier. This is a responsibility that supposes dependency, fidelity, and an activity in the name of the One represented. A modern exegete, a recognized authority on the Book of Genesis, makes a particularly pertinent comment. Referring to the command, "Fill the earth and subdue it: have dominion over the fishes of the sea, the birds of the sky" (Gn 1:28), he writes: "We regard the link between the concept of likeness to God and that of the task of exercising dominion as evident. After all, *selem* denotes a concrete copy: as the great ones of the earth cause their likenesses to be erected in the provinces of their kingdoms where they cannot go personally, as countersign of their principle of sovereignty, so also man, in his likeness to God, *is placed on this earth as a sign of the sovereignty of God.* Man is precisely God's legate, and is charged with the duty of safeguarding and extending the divine dominion over the earth" (Gerhard von Rad, *Genesis* [Brescia: Paideia], 172-173).

Accordingly, human beings carry about within themselves the whole seal of the dignity of the One they represent. Thus they act as God's vice-regents of all the goods placed in their hands by God. Herein resides the Thomistic conception of the right of disposition and administration in the name of God, the right to private ownership of the means of production. This right is a special call to responsibility, a call to direct all human activity and toil toward God.

4. The New Testament enrichment of the concrete theology of the meaning of the image: The human being is the image of God precisely in Christ, the perfect Image of the Father.

All must converge on the likeness to God—on our conformation (*conformes fieri*) to that Image of God *par excellence*, Christ. This assimilation, this "likening" to the Lord coincides with our authentic self-fulfillment. Our responsibility as human beings is not to disfigure this image that is our very dignity.

Christ, as *Redemptor Hominis* notes and as we have remarked, " '. . .fully reveals man to himself and brings to light his most high calling.' [He] is Himself the perfect man who has restored in the children of Adam that likeness to God which had been disfigured ever since the first sin" (*Redemptor Hominis*, 8). Herein is the rescue and restoration, the regeneration, wrought by the Redemption of Christ.

This eminent dignity, that of being the image of God, ultimately coincides with being a child of God. The child reproduces the image of the parent. Herein lies the revealed key of the *social being* of men and women, which corresponds to being members of God's family—persons who are called to be, and actually are, in Christ, *children of our heavenly Father*.

Hence the *transcendent character of the human person*, which is the source of our rights and obligations. Here is the root of the primacy of persons over structures, of our individual and social responsibility, our dignity, and the subjective value of human labor, which later is discussed by our Holy Father at length and with great clarity in his encyclical, *Laborem Exercens*. The human being must not be regarded as an anonymous element of society—one interchangeable part among many. The human being must not be regarded as a simple cog in the machinery of an economic or political system, or as a mere appendix thereof.

Inasmuch as the question of labor is the central theme of the social question, the dignity of the human being as image of God is basic to the social teaching of the Church. Thus in the magisterium of our Holy Father:

> Man has to subdue the earth and dominate it, because as the "image of God" he is a person, that is to say, a subjective being capable of acting in a planned and rational way, capable of deciding about himself, and with a tendency to self-realization. *As a person, man is therefore the subject of work.* . . . Human work has an ethical value of its own, which clearly and directly remains linked to the fact that the one who carries it out is a person, a conscious and free subject. . . . *The primary basis of the value of work is man himself.* (*Laborem Exercens*, 6; cf. 9)

There are numerous instances in the teaching of John Paul II in which this solid position of his, a position peculiar to Christian anthropology, is reiterated. Limitations of space oblige us to confine our considerations to a few such instances.

This teaching gleamed with a special luster in that scenario of pain and suffering where it would appear that hope had died, where there was only the painful spectacle of bodies ravaged by the dread disease of leprosy. Speaking to lepers in Marituba, Brazil, in the spirit of the proclamation of liberation issued by Jesus the Messiah, who heals the ills of humanity and goes in search of the prostrate, helpless human being, in that human being's "limit situation," to use Jaspers' expression, when men and woman can no longer help themselves, the Vicar of Christ bent low over human misery. His synthesis is penetrating: the human being is God's child, someone God loves. And he addressed the lepers as follows:

> And you, who are you? To me you are, first and foremost, human persons, rich with an immense dignity that bestows upon you the condition of person—rich, each of you, with a unique, matchless personal philosophy. This is how God made you. . . . You are children of God, known and loved by him. (Address in Marituba, Brazil, July 8, 1980, 3)

The human being is the *image of God* by virtue of being a *child of God*. *To farm workers*, in Recife, wallowing in their miserable marginality, he indicates what it means to be the image of God:

> The earth is man's because God has entrusted it to man. . . . The earth is a gift of God, a gift that he makes to all human beings, men and women, whom he wishes to see joined together in a single family, and relating to one another in a fraternal spirit. (Homily in Recife, July 7, 1980, 4)

And he adds that Christ "has taken sides with human dignity." In the human family, the marginalized must find a place at table. The human being is not merely a tool of production (cf. *ibid.,* 5, 6).

To the natives and campesinos, in Cuilapân, he recalls that they "have a right to effective help, which is neither a handout nor a few crumbs of justice, so that they may have access to the development that their dignity as human beings and as children of God merits" ("Address to the Indians of Oaxaca and

Chiapas," in *Puebla and Beyond*, 82). Accordingly, he insists that field workers "have a right not to be deprived of the little they have by maneuvers that sometimes amount to real plunder" (*ibid.*), and cries: "It is not just, it is not human, it is not Christian to continue certain situations that are clearly unjust" (*ibid.*, 83). From the vision of the human being in Christ, he passes directly to the principles of the social teaching of the Church and the requirements of its application.

To workers, in Sao Paulo, he indicates the task of *being the image of God by toil*: "Made in the image of God, [the human being] has received the mission of being the administrator of all things, in order to develop their wealth, and confer on them a universal destination — in order to join human beings together in mutual service and the creation of a worthy, beautiful system of life" (meeting with workers in Sao Paulo, July 3, 1980, 7).

To workers, in Monterrey, he had declared:

> I know that I am speaking to workers who are aware of their condition as Christians. . . . The pope therefore wishes to address to you certain reflections touching your dignity as human beings and as children of God. From this double font will spring the light to mold your personal and social existence. After all, if the Spirit of Christ dwells in us, we ought to feel a priority concern for those who have no suitable food, clothing, housing, or access to the goods of culture. (Address to the workers of Monterrey, January 31, 1979, 3)

To the leaders of poor parishes, in Medellín, the Holy Father explained how Christian dignity is perceived by the Church. It is this dignity that is at the basis of rights to be defended:

> You experience in the Church, in a special way, the dignity of children of God — the noblest, the loveliest title to which a human being can aspire. Keep this dignity alive and operative. In it resides the grandeur that the Church fosters, guards, and promotes. No one has as many reasons to love the poor, respect them, and demand respect for them, as has the Church. . . . In his dignity as a child of God is the root of every human being's rights, whose guarantor is God himself. The Church, therefore, obedient to the mandate it has received, urges upon us the duties of solidarity, justice,

and charity toward all, especially toward those most in need. (Meeting with priests working in the *barrios* of Medellín, July 5, 1986, 2, 3)

To youth, in Belo Horizonte, he proclaims the transcendent dimension of a human being "created to the likeness of God."

[That human being is] called to be God's child, and a brother and sister to other human beings. He or she is destined for eternal life. To deny this transcendence is to reduce the human being to a tool of domination, whose lot will now be that of a victim of the selfishness and ambition of other human beings, or of the omnipotence of a totalitarian state elevated to the status of supreme value. (Homily at the Mass for youth and students, Belo Horizonte, July 1, 1980, 4)

That this is a deep conviction of the heart and mind of John Paul II is clear as well from *Have No Fear—A Dialogue with John Paul II* (Milan, 1983):

There is no need to belabor the key role this notion [of the image of God] has played in anthropology and theology from the very earliest times. . . . Methods change, as do philosophical preferences, but the basis of biblical anthropology abides. . . . All this wealth of the human being evinces the fact that transcendence is a constitutive dimension of that being. By his very humanity, man is called to surpass himself. This fact, described in various manners, explains what is meant by the *image of God*.

Truly a basic idea of St. Leo the Great flourishes in the anthropological dimension of the papal magisterium today:

Acknowledge, O Christian, thy dignity, and inasmuch as thou dost now participate in the divine nature itself, return not to thy ancient baseness. . . . Remember of what Head and what Body thou art a member. Keep in mind that thou hast been snatched from the dominion of darkness and transported unto the Kingdom and brightness of God. (Sermon 1 on the Nativity of the Lord, 1, 3)

132

There has been a great deal of insistence on the original dignity of our first creation. As we know, however, our dignity in Christ is one of regeneration, of restoration to the likeness of God, in the conciliar formulation endorsed by John Paul II: "Christ, the final Adam. . .is Himself the perfect man. To the sons of Adam He restores the divine likeness which had been disfigured from the first sin onward" (*Redemptor Hominis*, 8; citing *Gaudium et Spes*, 22). In Christ we have a new existence, we are a new creation, through the mystery of regeneration (cf. Mt 19:28, Ti 3:5), which in John is a new birth (3:3-8), as it entails a share in the divine life.

The apostolic exhortation, *Reconciliatio et Paenitentia* is fairly steeped in this theme. From a description of a world in smithereens from the wound human beings have received in their deepest heart, the wound of sin, the Holy Father proceeds to the situation wrought by Christ the Reconciler in the *mysterium pietatis*: a reconciled life. God's love is ever faithful. Never will the heart of God be closed to the children of God. God seeks them, awaits them, goes out to meet them, wherever their rejection of communion renders them prisoners of isolation and division. "This initiative on God's part is made concrete and manifest in the redemptive act of Christ, which radiates through the world by means of the ministry of the Church" (*Reconciliatio et Paenitentia*, 10). From the *mysterium iniquitatis* he proceeds to the *mysterium* or *sacramentum pietatis*: "This same *mystery of God's infinite loving kindness towards us* is capable of penetrating to the hidden roots of our iniquity, in order to evoke in the soul a movement of conversion, in order to redeem it and set it on course towards reconciliation" (*ibid.*, 20).

In its theology of the image, this theological anthropology includes an admirable synthesis of the restoration of the likeness of God. The human being without Christ changes, becoming the human being with Christ:

> A new relationship with the immutable God is inconceivable without a change in man. This change is an effect of the divine activity, as well as the foundation of the new personal relationships established by man with the Holy Trinity in Jesus Christ. The renewal of this divine likeness must be considered under two aspects. Under the aspect of being, man becomes a partaker of the divine nature, or, as the Fathers say, is "divinized." Under the aspect of having,

man possesses the firstfruits of the Spirit—created grace. (Mauritio Flick and Zoltan Alszeghy, *Anthropologia teológica* [Salamanca: Sígueme, 1985], 401)

The truth about the human being as against the ideologies

By virtue of the transcendent dimension of the human person, the human being is not, and must not be, a tool or cog in the machinery of the ideologies. There is no need for recourse to systems or ideologies in order to love, defend, and cooperate in the liberation of the human being (cf. John Paul II, "Opening Address at Puebla," II, 2, 65).

The Holy Father's remarks on conceptualizations like those of Hobbes, Rousseau, and Hegel himself, are profound and carefully composed:

> With humanity's wounding by sin, our internal unity has been sundered. Estranging itself from God's friendship, man's heart has become a place of torment and conflict, a veritable battleground. Tortured and divided within himself, man is estranged from his neighbors. It is not in God's original plan, however, for man to be an enemy to man— *homo homini lupus.* Man was intended to be brother to man. God's design reveals a dialectic not of confrontation, but of a love that makes all things new, a love flowing from the spiritual rock that is Christ. (Homily, "Peace and Reconciliation," 2)

Here we have a radically different anthropology from the Marxist conception of the human being, according to which it is the possession of the means of production or the lack thereof— *economic alienation*—that divides human beings internally and separates them from one another. Here is the root of the concept of *conflictivity*, which derives from a conception of the human being as essentially immersed in struggle—a conception so different from the Christian notion, in which a communion of brothers and sisters, the social being of humanity, belongs to God's original plan. Human beings are not at the mercy of structures, or of economic or political systems. Nor are they subject to the process of class struggle, as in Marxist revolutionary praxis.

The pope does not deny the influence of structures, or the conditions that proceed from these structures, on human beings. He is not unmindful of the evils inflicted on humanity by a *rigid capitalism* or a *Marxist collectivism*. His is a different conception of the human being, one of personal worth and dignity. Even before *Reconciliatio et Paenitentia*, the pope defined the content of "social sin," so admirably, as "the evil that penetrates hearts and social structures. The evil of division among men, which has sown a world of tombs with its wars, with this terrible spiral of hatred, razes and annihilates, sullenly, senselessly" ("Peace and Reconciliation," 3). The Holy Father is thinking of the long, cruel, violent drama of El Salvador.

In John Paul II's magisterium, love, not struggle, and not the more or less masked forms of hatred that accompany struggle, has the last word. It is ethically impermissible "to elevate hatred to such a position that it becomes confounded with the nobility of a cause, and even confused with a restorative, healing act of love" (*ibid.*). He denounces this "terrible chain reaction, proper to the dialectic of friend and enemy" (*ibid.,* 5), and counterposes the difficult, heroic commandment to love our enemies—yes, and forgive them.

The human person is not simply the victim of structures, to the detriment of any personal responsibility. Nor may we accept a tenuous, will-o'-the-wisp conception of "social sin" such that "sin, in its genuine and proper sense" would no longer be "an act of the person, since it is a free act of the individual person, and not precisely that of a group or community. A man can be conditioned, pressured, driven by more than a few powerful external factors, as he can also be influenced by the tendencies, defects, and customs of his social state. . . . But it is a truth of faith, confirmed as well by our experience and reason, that the human person is free" (*ibid.,* 16). The concept of social sin authentically refers to "solidarity" in sin. Our sin has repercussions on our neighbors. The concept of social sin authentically refers to the direct assault of certain sins on persons, and to sins committed against justice in interpersonal relationships, among individuals as between individuals and society (cf. *Reconciliatio et Paenitentia*, 16).

This position is fully consistent with that of the *Instruction on Christian Freedom and Liberation* published by the Congregation for the Doctrine of the Faith, according to which persons have priority over structures, and in which we are invited to "act for the conversion of hearts as well as for the improvement of structures" (*ibid.*, 75).

Christian anthropology, the option for the poor, and liberation

From a point of departure in the truth concerning the human being, we arrive at the most significant element in the social teaching of the Church, and concretely, at a Christian liberation praxis in a *preferential* love (the meaning of the "option" for the poor) for our least, neediest sisters and brothers.

The pope warns:

> The Church of the poor speaks first and foremost of every man. . . . It is not the Church of a class or social caste. . . . The Church of the poor has no wish to serve political ends or power struggles. Indeed it strives most assiduously to keep its words and actions from being utilized for a like end—from being manipulated. (Visit to the Vidigal slum, Rio de Janeiro, July 2, 1980, 5)

Speaking in Haiti, the pope addresses the bishops of Latin America:

> The very poorest must find a preference in your fatherly hearts and your pastoral solicitude. Therefore you know and proclaim that a like option would be neither pastoral nor Christian were it to be inspired in mere political or ideological criteria, were it to be exclusive or excluding, or if it were to foment feelings of hatred, or a struggle among brothers. (Address to the Assembly of the Latin American Bishops Conference, March 9, 1983, 3)

He recalls that "the best service to one's brothers is evangelization, which disposes them to fulfill themselves as children of God" (address to the Latin American Bishops Conference, Rio de Janeiro, July 2, 1980, 7).

As for liberation, the nub of the controversy has been whether to have recourse to Marxist analysis or to the social teaching of the Church, which rebels against ideologies. More concretely, the discussion is centered on whether or not to appeal to a "class struggle." For the liberationists of Marxist inspiration, *the class struggle is a massive, undeniable fact*, and one simply must take sides. For those who follow the broad, clear lines of the magisterium, the class struggle is an ideological option—an interpretation rather than a fact, itself a form of struggle, and unacceptable to the consistent Christian.

The particular modality of the theology of liberation that is criticized here was in the process of voiding, sterilizing the Church.

Violence only destroys. This document enjoyed the broadest possible world diffusion. What must be, and is, the nub of the controversy? Not love for the poor, which the Church has amply demonstrated. What is in dispute, what is unacceptable, what is categorically rejected by the bishops of Colombia and other parts of the continent, was and continues to be the Marxist inspiration of certain currents, and their illicit use of its categories.

The inappropriate use of these categories, centered on a *class struggle*, had already been denounced. These deviations were denounced even by theologians sympathetic to more moderate approaches, such as Schillebeeckx, Moltmann, and not a few Latin Americans. The Puebla Conference would soon issue a forthright warning of the danger to the Church lurking in the more extreme approaches. The evil was metastasizing, and destroying the harmony of theological reflection. As the bishops declared at Puebla:

> We must also note the risk of ideologization run by theological reflection when it is based on a praxis that has recourse to Marxist analysis. The consequences are the total politicization of Christian existence, the disintegration of the language of faith into that of the social sciences, and the draining away of the transcendental dimension of Christian salvation. ("Puebla Final Document" 545, in *Puebla and Beyond*, 200)

The Puebla Conference incorporated into its "discernment for liberation in Christ" Paul VI's categorical admonition:

> The Church would lose her fundamental meaning. Her message of liberation would no longer have any originality and would easily be open to monopolization and manipula-

tion by ideological systems and political parties. (*Evangelii Nuntiandi*, 32)

That we were not mistaken is shown by the Holy Father's words to the Colombian bishops:

Bear genuine hope to the poor, who, inspired by their supernatural faith, look to the Church as their sole defense. . . . Blaze trails of hope and authentic liberation, along the lines of your episcopal document, *Christian Identity in Activity for Justice*, and the teaching of the magisterium. . .as you continue to toil, dear brothers, in the closest union, for the authentic liberation that comes to us from Jesus Christ, the Redeemer of Man, which must be defended from ideologies alien to it, ideologies that evacuate its evangelical content. (Address to the Colombian Episcopate, 8)

The solidarity of the bishops in this matter has perhaps been stronger in Colombia than in other parts of our continent.

On August 6, 1974, the Congregation for the Doctrine of the Faith saw itself under the necessity of publishing, with the approval of the Holy Father, the exhortation, *Libertatis Nuntius: On Certain Aspects of the Theology of Liberation*. The purpose of the document was to expose the current distortions and serious errors being committed in the name of faith and pastoral ministry. *All* of the Latin American bishops' conferences accepted it, and this in writing, in documents dispatched to the Holy See.

And a second document was announced, which, we learned, would indicate positive pathways to an authentic liberation. The latter — a lengthy, extremely precise and detailed work, the fruit of seven drafts, as well as previous consultation with the bishops' conferences of the world — appeared on March 22, 1986, in the form of an Instruction of the Congregation for the Doctrine of the Faith entitled *Libertatis Conscientia*. It, too, was issued with the approval of the Holy Father.

The pope had shared this second document with a group of Brazilian bishops at their meeting in Rio de Janeiro from March 13 to 15. In his address of March 13, he asked for "a definition of the evangelical and ecclesial identity" of liberation theology. And he continued: "Purified of elements that might adulterate it, with grave consequences for the faith, the theology of liberation is not only orthodox, but necessary." Let us take careful note: *Purified*—that is, with the errors of some of the currents corrected in accordance with what had been expressed in the exhortation, *Libertatis Nuntius*, which retains its *full validity*. The second document, *Libertatis Conscientia*, declares: "Far from being superseded, the warnings already issued *appear ever more opportune and pertinent*." Could anything be clearer?

Has there been some change in John Paul's position with regard to the theology of liberation? Is it true that what the Holy See once corrected and censured has now been approved, accepted, and granted full citizenship? It is curious how insistently and enthusiastically some have suggested that John Paul II has "taken a different tack lately."

In the first place, the Holy Father has never rejected an authentic *Christian* liberation, whose font and source is Jesus Christ. The Church's rejection regards certain misguided theologies of liberation.

What does the pope write to the bishops of Brazil after the conclusion of their three-day meeting? In the letter delivered to the bishops by Cardinal Gantin, Prefect of the Congregation for Bishops, we read:

> The numerous documents published lately, among them the two recent Instructions of the Congregation for the Doctrine of the Faith, which carry my explicit approval, abundantly evince the close attention with which we follow these same efforts. . . . To the extent that it strives to find these correct answers—answers steeped in an understanding of the rich experience of the Church in this country, responses as effective and constructive as can be, and at the same time *in harmony and consistency with the teachings of the Gospel, living tradition, and the perennial magisterium of the Church*, we are convinced, you as well as I, that the theology of liberation is not only appropriate, but useful and necessary. It must constitute a new step— strictly connected with the preceding steps—in that theological reflection that began with the apostolic tradition and that has continued with the great Fathers and Doctors, with the ordinary and extraordinary magisterium, and, in more recent times, with the rich legacy of the social teaching of the Church. . . .

And he adds:

> Liberation is first and foremost soteriological [an aspect of the salvation wrought by Jesus Christ, the Son of God]. Only secondarily is it ethico-social [or sociopolitical]. To reduce one dimension to the other has the practical effect of canceling both. To reverse their proper order is to subvert and eviscerate authentic Christian liberation.

Indeed:

> May God assist you to exercise constant vigilance, that a *correct* and necessary theology of liberation may develop in Brazil and throughout Latin America *in a homogenous, and not a heterogeneous, manner* vis-à-vis the theology of all times, in complete loyalty to the teaching of the Church. (#5)

My purpose in transcribing these texts has been to preclude the least doubt as to the Holy Father's actual intent. Clearly, that intent is to purify liberation to the point where it is *worthy to be called Christian*. This is no easy task, when to the ears of the uninformed, "liberation theology" may now have a negative connotation. In other words, as the Secretary of the Latin American Bishops Conference has aptly noted, "in the Holy Father's beautiful letter to the bishops of Brazil, the Church has recovered and rehabilitated the term, 'theology of liberation,' which certain persons had appropriated to themselves." What is important is its content—fidelity to the truth we are given in the Church.

There has been no change in the pope's teaching. Quite to the contrary. The pope delves deep into its concerns and hopes, and invites the many bishops of Brazil to work along these same lines, just as he invited the Colombian episcopate to "continue working for authentic liberation."

To the members of the Latin American Bishops Conference, with respect to the pair of documents from the Holy See just mentioned, he indicates: "In the framework of the pontifical magisterium, you have contributed to a more precise definition of the authentic evangelical sense of *basic concepts that have been arbitrarily presented from an ideological, classist point of view.* . . ." Alluding to his letter to the Brazilian Bishops Conference, he states: "While acknowledging the utility and necessity of the theology of liberation, I wished to recall, as well, that it *must develop in harmony and continuity with the theological tradition of the Church and in conformity with its social teaching.*"

All of this is precisely noticeable by its absence, according to the Holy See itself, in numerous writings of certain currents of liberation theology. Further: the animadversions addressed to certain authors by the Doctrine of the Faith retain all of their validity and clarity.

Speaking to a throng of leaders of poor, working-class parishes in Medellín, the Holy Father spoke as follows:

> The Church may in no wise allow the banner of justice to be snatched from its hands by any ideology or political current. . . . The Colombian Church, for its part, has sought to be at the service of the poor, and does not cease to ratify this commitment.

Solidarity, says the pope, "will be the fruit of the noble struggle for justice, which is not a struggle of brother with brother, or of group against group, but must ever be imbued with the evangelical principles of collaboration and dialogue, to the exclusion, then, of every form of violence."

What, then, can underlie certain theses maintained by Christians for Socialism and the Popular Church to the effect that there could ever be harmony between Marxists and Christians, or that one must employ the Marxist analysis? One even hears that the pope has changed his mind! All of which is the sheerest nonsense.

The priests of Colombia enthusiastically applauded this fine synthesis by John Paul II, herald of liberation in Jesus Christ:

> But the options and the illumination Christians need in the area of human promotion and liberation, especially that of the very neediest, can only be made according to the example of Jesus and obtained in the light of the Gospel, which forbids recourse to methods of hatred and violence. Love, and a preferential option for the poor, must not be exclusive or excluding. Love for the poor does not mean

regarding the poor as a class, let alone as a class caught up in a struggle, or as a Church separated from communion with and obedience to the shepherds appointed for them by Christ. Love, and the preferential option for the poor, must be implemented in the context of a conceptualization of the human being in his earthly and eternal calling.

This is the viewpoint — so characteristic of the Holy Father's social conception — from which he spoke so emphatically in his address, "Christ in the World of Work," which he delivered in El Tunal Park:

> The social teaching of the Church inspires Christian praxis in its noble struggle for justice. But it excludes, as foreign to the Gospel, *a programmed class struggle*, which only leads to new forms of servitude. (#348)

The Holy Father remarked the fact that peace, among peoples as well as within individual nations, is only attained by way of reconciliation. There is never any actual, authentic liberation without reconciliation, and the latter finds its concretization in forgiveness, the original act of Christian love (cf. *Dives in Misericordia*), and in true conversion. Commenting on the episode of Jesus in the Synagogue at Nazareth, the Holy Father teaches:

> The Gospel passage just proclaimed contains a synthesis of that message of Messianic liberation that comports *the entire mystery of reconciliation*, whose supreme realization passes by way of the cross. ("Christ Our Reconciliation," address in Barranquilla, 724)

And he adds:

> The message of *liberation and reconciliation in Christ* is projected into the "today" of our existence as a light empowering us to execute a profound analysis of the reality

of our world, in which sin and its consequences of oppression and injustice become present. (#29)

Alfonso Cardinal López Trujillo
Archbishop of Medellín
(Colombia)

(Translated from Spanish by Robert R. Barr)

HUMAN WORK IN THE TEACHING OF OUR HOLY FATHER JOHN PAUL II

Jozef Cardinal Glemp

I. THE VICAR OF CHRIST KNOWS FROM HIS OWN EXPERIENCE WHAT WORK IS

The concrete experience of human work is enshrined in John Paul II's social teaching. Thanks to this fact, theoretical reflection has, in that teaching, found a valid foundation in the practical side of life. On a personal level, the pope has deeply grasped, has "sweated out" directly the problems concerning labor, both physical and mental, the work done in mines and factories, scientific and artistic work, theological and pastoral work. His biography is that of a man who has worked unceasingly, and worked hard. "I do not hesitate to say that the following four years, spent among laboring folk, were for me a gift of Providence. The experience I acquired during that period of my life was priceless. I have often stated that perhaps I have given to these years a higher value than to a doctorate; which, of course, does not mean that I undervalue university degrees" (A. Froissard, *Giovanni Paulo II* [Milan, 1983], 13-14).

Elsewhere, the pope admits: "Thanks to my personal experience I can affirm that the gospel appears to me in a new light" (homily at workers' gathering, Conception, April 5, 1987).

Let us keep in mind that the one who speaks thus is the Vicar of Christ, of that Christ who, "for the greater part of his life was a working man" (homily to workers, Ciudad Guayana, January 29, 1985), that "He Himself was a man of work, a craftsman like Joseph of Nazareth" (*Laborem Exercens*, 26). In this manner, too, through sharing in this work, we can achieve, thanks to the action of Providence, the "following of Christ." The Holy Father gives us, in fact, a living example of this.

II. THE ROOTS OF THE "GOSPEL OF LABOR" IN THE LIGHT OF HOLY SCRIPTURE

This conviction, that work constitutes the fundamental dimension of the person's existence on this earth, is one that the Church draws from that source which is the revealed word of God. This obvious truth appears already on the first pages of Genesis. "When man, who had been created 'in the image of God. . . male and female' (Gn 1:27), hears the words: 'Be fruitful and multiply; fill the earth and subdue it' (Gn 1:28) even though these words do not refer directly and explicitly to work, beyond a doubt they indicate it indirectly, as an activity for man to carry out in the world. Indeed, they show its deepest essence. Man is the image of God, partly through the mandate received from his Creator to subdue and dominate the earth. In carrying out this commission, man, every human being, reflects the very action of the Creator of the Universe" (*Laborem Exercens*, 4).

According to the pope's teaching, the very act of creation gives rise to the essential consequences of man's ulterior destiny. Work lies at the very root of man's future, when this was "entrusted" to him as his task by the Creator. "God called man to existence, and at the same time established him as master 'over the works of his hands, placing everything at his feet,' as we read in Psalm 8:7. From the most remote times God is represented to us as the 'Maker,' as the One who does things; and he has entrusted his own work as a heritage to man, so that he might take care of it and use it for his own life and development. Man's creative familiarity with the work of creation finds its expression in all forms of work, material or intellectual, in the work of the artisan, in industry, in service enterprises and in cultural activities. Work. . . manifests man's resemblance to God, and by so doing constitutes the indispensable foundation of human dignity. The Son of God himself became man in a family of working people; he learned to be an artisan, and called as his disciples men belonging to the working class" (to workers, May 2, 1987).

By original sin man wrecked that plan of God's even though he did not entirely destroy it. After he had broken his first covenant with God, man heard the words: "In the sweat of thy brow shalt thou eat bread" (Gn 3:19). But did this mean, perhaps, that from then on work would be only a curse, a burden, a punishment? Certainly not. In his infinite mercy God led man by the hand in such a way that through work and love the spoiled harmony might be reestablished. Instead of seeing work as a curse, we must look upon it above all as an invitation to man to share in the task of Christ's Redemption, which he took upon himself for the salvation of humanity. "Jesus who works," teaches John Paul II in Colombia, "is for you the most eloquent 'gospel of work.' Is it not a source of comfort, a stimulus and an encouragement, this vision of the Son of God who becomes man and who by the work of his hands, earns what he needs to live? Look at him; although he was God, 'he emptied himself, taking on the role of a servant' (Ph 2:7), to redeem work from within" (to the *barrios* of Bogota, July 3, 1986).

In this way the insertion of human work into the task of redeeming the world gives a new meaning to fatigue, to weariness, to any difficulty, which, "united with the Passion of Christ, the Redeemer of man, becomes a means of salvation for each one and for all" (*ibid.*). Man, worn out by his daily work, collaborates in a certain measure with Christ, and helps him carry his cross. "He shows himself a true disciple of Christ by carrying the cross in his turn every day, in the activity he is called upon to accomplish" (*Laborem Exercens*, 27).

The Holy Father who belongs so thoroughly to the world of labor and to that of culture, often quotes the meaningful words of his compatriot, the great poet K. Norwid: "Work is. . . to rise again" (homily at Czestochowa, June 6, 1979). Because in labor "precisely, thanks to the light that penetrates us from the Resurrection of Christ, we always find a glimpse of new light, of a new good, as it were an announcement of the new heaven and the new earth (cf. 2 P 3:13), in which man and the world participate, precisely through the toil that goes with work" (*Laborem Exercens*, 27).

In a fuller and more expressive manner the pope presented the link between work and Resurrection in one of his homilies in Chile: "The Resurrection is the sign of that deep meaning found in human labor, and the Resurrection joined with labor. Labor does not lead to death, but to the Resurrection. It is a marvelous coincidence that the liturgy of the fifth Sunday in Lent should speak to us of the resurrection of Lazarus. It is a providential coincidence. In the context of this event, the Lord Jesus addresses himself to the world of labor, to the working people of Chile. There is no divergence here; for the deepest human and Christian implications of labor are seen all the better precisely through the Resurrection of Christ; and through sharing in the cross of Christ we come to the Resurrection" (homily, Conception, April 5, 1987).

Basically, all of holy scripture, beginning with the books of the Old Testament, constitutes the basic "gospel of work"; it still remains the living and irreplaceable starting point and reference point for contemporary theological reflection on the question of human work. In the same way, the social doctrine of the Church — including the teaching of John Paul II — stands on that lasting foundation. In fact, down the ages, there has been no change in the proclamation of the Good News — the meaning of evangelization, in which the meaning of work has remained unaltered. As Christ has joined the work of salvation to his work in the shop at Nazareth, so too John Paul II has joined evangelization with physical labor. "The Church in our day needs very specially this apostolate of the working class; the apostolate of the workers, and the apostolate among the laboring classes, to enlighten once more with the light of the gospel this important sector of life" (to workers at Mayence, November 16, 1980).

In still more expressive terms the Holy Father repeated this truth to the workers at Mistrzejowice-Nowa Huta: "Christ entrusted his gospel to the hands and hearts of the fishermen from the lake of Genesareth; and today you must take it into your hands and hearts so that it may be preached to every creature, so that the man in industry, the man of today's technical civilization, may find in it himself, his dignity and his rights" (June 22, 1983).

III. LABOR, THE CONSTANT OBJECT OF THE CHURCH'S MAGISTERIUM

John Paul II's social teaching, and thus also his "gospel of work" for the world of today, springs from the very roots of holy scripture, and takes its place in the constant teaching of the Church, thus enriching and developing the reflections contained in the great social encyclicals of the nineteenth and twentieth centuries, as well as in other documents of the Church, and in particular, the huge treasure of the Acts of Vatican II. The pope, in the pursuit of his teaching mission, is in a certain way the natural heir and the continuator of this patrimony which he has constantly enriched. Almost at the start of his pontificate during his "first official meeting with the world of work" (discourse to the workers at Pomezia, September 13, 1979), the Holy Father referred directly to the social encyclicals like *Rerum Novarum* of Leo XIII, *Quadragesimo Anno* of Pius XI, *Mater et Magistra*, and *Pacem in Terris* of John XXIII, as well as *Populorum Progressio* of Paul VI.

The pope recalled the statements made by John XXIII and Paul VI in his first encyclical, *Redemptor Hominis*. It deals basically with the mystery of the Redemption, but at the same time it contains the affirmation that at the heart of these reflections the social question must be placed, and together with it, the fundamental problem of work (cf. *Redemptor Hominis*, 16).

Soon afterwards, that promise was realized, first with his next encyclical, *Dives in Misericordia*, where the Holy Father takes up the above-mentioned problem, viewed in the light of God's mercy (#s 2, 5, 11, 12). Then, on September 14, 1981, John Paul II published a new fundamental encyclical, *Laborem Exercens*, entirely dedicated to human labor, and published, as the subtitle indicates, on the occasion of the ninetieth anniversary of *Rerum Novarum*. "This historical reference situates the papal document in the logical and coherent continuity of the tradition, which began, precisely, with *Rerum Novarum* and embraces the almost century-long patrimony of the Church's social doctrine. Out of this same source does the work of John Paul II arise, his Letter on Human Labor."

The reasons which led to the writing of this Letter were explained by the pope himself on various occasions. "At a period in which the world is torn by conflicts of various kinds, and filled with contradictions; when injustice in its many aspects rules; and when there reigns an improper division of goods which gives rise to tensions and struggles, the pope could not fail to publish an encyclical on human work. The gospel of work and of peace had to be proclaimed with special energy" (to the people of God in the diocese of Szezscin-Kamien, Czestochowa, June 18, 1983).

The Holy Father enumerates these reasons in particular, in the introduction to his encyclical. The Letter constitutes, in the first place, an answer to the challenge, not only of the present times, but of those which will follow. "We are celebrating the ninetieth anniversary of the encyclical *Rerum Novarum* on the eve of new developments in technological, economic and political conditions which will influence the world of work and of production no less than did the industrial revolution of the last century" (*Laborem Exercens*, 1). Such changes regard the great development of various techniques: from automation to the rise in the price of energy and of raw material, along with the escalation of threats to the ecology. In addition, the urgent problems of the unemployed, the tragic inequality of wealth and of the distribution of wealth, and of opportunities, whether on the local level or on a worldwide scale, and finally the question of the aspirations of people who, "after centuries of subjection, are demanding their rightful place among the nations and in international decision making" (*ibid.*).

In these ten years of the current pontificate, the encyclical *Laborem Exercens* constitutes undoubtedly a most competent document of the Church's supreme magisterium regarding the so-called social question, understood in its broadest terms. All the successive statements of the pope consider this document as a fundamental point of reference. Nonetheless, the social teaching of John Paul II, in these years 1978-88 should be considered as a harmonic whole, the hub of which certainly remains the encyclical on human work, just as "human work constitutes the key to social life" (to Polish bishops, October 11, 1982) and "occupies the central position in the social question" (*Laborem Exercens*, 3).

IV. SUBJECTIVE CHARACTER OF WORK,
THE KEY TO SOCIAL LIVING

We have already mentioned that for the Holy Father all work possesses a triple dimension: divine, through the work of creation and the act of salvation; and then human, whether individual or social. In the tersest manner possible the Holy Father expressed this triple dimension of "the Christian concept of work," when he was at Sao Paulo: "It begins with faith in God the Creator, and then, through Christ the Redeemer, arrives at the construction of human society, at solidarity with men. Without this vision, every effort, even the most tenacious, is not sufficient, and will ultimately fail" (to workers at Sao Paulo, July 3, 1980).

In the human dimension, the foundation of such a vision resides in the dignity and the subjectivity of man, and what flows therefrom: the subjectivity of the work he performs. The pope thus clarifies this basic view. "As the image of God, man is a person, that is to say, a subjective being, capable of acting in a planned and rational way, capable of deciding about himself and with a tendency to self-realization. As a person, man therefore is the subject of work" (*Laborem Exercens*, 6). From this truth there flows also a fundamental consequence, ethical in nature: "However true it may be that man is destined for work and called to it, in the first place work is 'for' man, and not man 'for work' " (*ibid.*). Thus, man is either "the primary basis of the value of work" or he is its ultimate end. Notwithstanding all its burdensomeness work is, at the same time, a good for man; a good that corresponds with his natural dignity, in that, precisely through work, "he affirms himself as a man and in a certain way becomes more fully a man" (*ibid.*). In his address to the International Labor Organization the pope again clarified the essence of this connection: "The connection between work and human existence itself, always bears testimony to the fact that man is not alienated by work, is not enslaved by it. On the contrary, it reiterates that work has become the ally of his humanity; it helps to live in truth and liberty, a liberty built on truth, which permits him to live more fully a life more worthy of man" (to the ILO, Geneva, June 15, 1982).

It is not only the state of man as a subject which was often questioned in the course of human history. In the process of his being made a thing and degraded, work too was undervalued. True, humanity has left behind the phenomenon of slavery, which offended and degraded the dignity of man, and at the same time the work performed by the slave; but many other forms of slavery persist even in our day. The patent injustices in the field of labor relations, so characteristic of the period of industrialization in the nineteenth century, provoked a reaction, morally well founded, on the part of all the laboring classes, who were being exploited, thus causing the so-called "worker question" to take on a historical role. As time went on these dilemmas were indeed resolved to a great extent, a result to which the Church and her social teaching made no small contribution. However, the question has not yet been completely settled – the historic conflict between the world of labor and the world of capital remains. In this conflict the Church declares herself logically in favor of the priority of labor over capital. "This principle directly concerns the process of production; in this process labor is always a primary efficient cause, while capital – the whole collection of means of production — remains a mere instrument, or instrumental cause. . . . This gigantic and powerful instrument — the whole collection of means of production that in a sense is considered synonymous with 'capital' is the result of work and bears the imprint of human labor. . . . We must emphasize and give prominence to the primacy of man in the production process, the primacy of man over things. Everything contained in the concept of capital in the strict sense is only a collection of things. Man, as the subject of work, and independently of the work that he does, alone is a person. This truth has important and decisive consequences" (*Laborem Exercens*, 12).

In the history of human thought labor was separated from capital because of two kinds of errors: economic and materialistic. The mentality weighed down by these errors subjected to material reality all the spirituality of work, and the personal dimension which belongs to it, namely, that of the subject who performs it. "There does not exist," affirms John Paul II, "any other possibility of eliminating the consequences of those errors except the patient construction of the foundation of a just system of work which overcomes in its very basis the opposition between labor and capital, through an effort at being shaped in accordance with the principle. . . of the substantial and real priority of labor, of the subjectivity of human labor, and its effective participation in the whole production process" (*Laborem Exercens*, 13).

The Church's social teaching, from Leo XIII to John Paul II has never accepted either the theory or the practice of considering the world of labor as an object, through greedy "economic capitalism" which absolutizes the category of profit and debases the dignity of human work; at the same time her teaching does not agree, either, with the false promise of Marxism, with the possibility of overcoming the conflict between labor and capital through the elimination of private property. "Thus, merely converting the means of production into state property in the collectivist system, is by no means equivalent to 'socializing' that property. We can speak of socialization only when the subjective character of society is insured, that is to say, when on the basis of his work each person is fully entitled to consider himself a part-owner of the great workbench at which he labors along with everyone else" (*Laborem Exercens*, 14). This point of view respects one's right to own private property, honestly gained. The means of proprietorship, and in particular the means of production, "cannot be possessed against labor; they cannot even be possessed for possession's sake, because the only legitimate title to their possession — whether in the form of private ownership or in the form of public or collective ownership — is that they should serve labor, and thus, by serving labor, that they should make possible the achievement of the first principle of this order, namely, the universal destination of goods, and the right to common use of them" (*ibid.*). On the other hand, observes the pope, "radically separating labor from property arouses concern" (to the United Nations, New York, October 2, 1979), given that every man needs to see that "within the production process some provision be made for him to be able to know that in his work, even on something that is owned in common, he is working for himself" (*Laborem Exercens*, 15).

This individual and personalistic aspect of human labor does not at all hide its social and communitarian dimension. "It is characteristic of work that first and foremost it unites people. In this consists its social power: the power to build a community" (*ibid.*, 20). In the first place we have the community of the family, to provide for which labor is necessary. "Work, and industriousness also influence the whole process of education in the family, for the very reason that everyone becomes a human being through (among other things), work. The family is simultaneously a community made possible by work, and the first school of work, within the home, for every person" (*ibid.*, 10).

The "larger society" namely the nation, is the next, and equally important community of labor. To this community John Paul II attributes a basic significance. "It is a great historical and social incarnation of the work of all generations. All of this brings it about that man combines his deepest human identity with membership in a nation, and intends his work also to increase the common good developed together with his compatriots, thus realizing that in this way work serves to add to the heritage of the whole human family" (*ibid.*).

Every country, every nation, is essentially one great workbench, as the Holy Father has explained it, taking his own nation as an example. "Poland is a great field of work, a field of human labor, of Polish labor, composed of many productive sections. I am referring to work, including intellectual work: to work in factories and to the work of the entire people; to the work of professionals and to work done in the families, the work of fathers and mothers. It is this work on matter which man transforms so that it may supply his needs, but it is also the work of man, precisely that which begins in the heart of each mother and next to that heart, and which then lasts for all the life of the family and evolves through the years of education in schools, and beyond. What an enormous field of labor she is, our motherland!" (to delegates of Solidarnosc, Vatican, January 18, 1981).

And finally, it is through work that the sovereignty of the nation expresses itself, and also its subjective element. "Only then does a nation live a life of its own when in the entire organization of the state it affirms its own subjective character, and is sovereign in itself, contributing to this by its own labor and its own efforts. It is truly essential for the life of society that man should not lose confidence in his own work, but that he should realize the role that labor confers on him; that in his work, and through it, he should be acknowledged as a man: he, his family, and his convictions" (to the representatives of the Popular Republic of Poland, Warsaw, August 6, 1987).

Human labor forms communities, beginning with the family and all the way on up to the nation and the state.

V. RIGHTS AND DUTIES OF THE WORKING WORLD

The rights of the laboring man are viewed by John Paul II as organically bound up with the proper rights of the person. As yet it is not possible to treat of such rights separated from the fundamental duties of man, which, as a laboring man, he has with regard to God, others, and finally the human communities in which he has grown up. "Work is. . . an obligation, that is to say, a duty on the part of man. This is true in all the many meanings of the word. Man must work both because the Creator has commanded it, and because of his own humanity. . . which requires work in order to be maintained and developed. Man must work out of regard for others, especially his own family, but also for the society he belongs to, the country of which he is a citizen, and the whole human family of which he is a member, since he is the heir to the work of generations, and at the same time must share in building the future of those who will come after him in the course of history. All this constitutes the moral obligation of work, understood in its broad sense" (*Laborem Exercens*, 16).

The rights of the working man underlie, and, as the pope points out, "are the key element in the whole of the social moral order." These rights must be respected both by the "direct employers" with whom the workers bargain and contract directly, and by the "indirect employers." By this term we should understand the structure of the system of work, as defined by various institutions, such as the state, international or transnational companies, and also all the other forms of organizations which go beyond direct employers.

Among all the rights belonging to the working man, the first is the right to work, that is, "the issue of suitable employment for all who are capable of it," to which is opposed unemployment, which "in all cases is an evil, and which when it reaches a certain level, can become a real social disaster" (*ibid.*).

The Holy Father treats of remedying unemployment under whatever form, "as the most urgent duty among the categories of moral imperatives" (*ibid.,* 17). This obligation binds everyone, but especially the "indirect employers." In this area there are no miraculous formulas which can guarantee an easy and quick solution to such a difficult problem; but there do exist instead a number of means and measures which can, even if only gradually, bring about an improvement in the situation. Towards this should tend a rational coordination of the policy of employment, in the framework of which "the initiatives of individuals, free groups and local work centers and complexes must be safeguarded" (*ibid.,* 18). The Church's social teaching also recommends the improvement and the specialization of professional training, taking into consideration the constant changes in the various fields of production and of the labor market. We ought to mention also the re-defining of the credit system and the notion of developing the idea of solidarity. The Holy Father often addresses political men, industrialists and economists from all over the world, inviting them to create new jobs, and calling to their attention the degrading consequences, moral, psychological, and social, of unemployment, especially with regard to the young who are frustrated by the lack of opportunities which leads them to fall into many forms of dependence, and which degrades their dignity. The representative of the Holy See, speaking to the Conference of Labor Ministers of European countries, called attention, in 1986, to the following suggestions and proposals tending to reduce unemployment: 1) to limit the privileges of certain groups which hold back the process of creating new employment opportunities; 2) in the name of solidarity of conscience, not to allow nationalistic selfishness to enter into play; 3) to renew collaboration with the countries of the south, which would favor a positive influx even on the labor market in Europe; 4) to verify all the possibilities which can be found in the non-commercial sector, or which are not subject to the laws of the marketplace; 5) to adopt a shorter work day (cf. Conference of Labor Ministers of Europe, Madrid, January 20, 1986).

The right to a just salary is the final fundamental claim of the working man. "The justice of a socioeconomic system. . . is to be evaluated by the way in which man's work is properly remunerated" (*Laborem Exercens*, 19).

By a just remuneration we must understand, in practice, the remuneration which under the form of "family wage" of "family bonuses" of "maternity bonuses," and so on, will suffice for establishing and maintaining properly a family, and for providing for its future security (*ibid.*). In a specially explicit manner, John Paul II stresses the need for efforts for "a social re-evaluation of the mother's role" (*ibid.*). The work of women, consequently, "must be always and everywhere referred expressly to the vocation of women as wives and mothers of families," which constitutes "its superior value, compared with all other public tasks and works" (to workers at Uniontex, Lodz, June 13, 1987). In a word, there is no more important work.

In the same way the other rights of the working man should be respected, such as the right to the many social benefits dealing with the protection of the lives and health of workers, among these medical benefits and those aimed at promoting safety at work. Again, there is a right to rest — with special concern for Sunday. "The right to a pension, to insurance for old age, and against accidents connected with the workplace" (*ibid.,* 22). All these rights as the pope stresses, "are a moral requirement which binds in conscience, even in those cases in which current legislation has not yet been able to formulate them effectively with the help of legislative norms" (to worker groups, Quito, January 30, 1985).

With equal solicitude the Holy Father deals with other situations concerning the world of work, which present themselves, from the start, without those opportunities which belong to workers in general. He refers here to those persons in particular who are handicapped, yet who should not be "cut off from the working world" (*Laborem Exercens*, 22). The same should be said about "children deprived of protection, and forced to seek work" (message for the twentieth World Peace Day, December 8, 1986). He also refers to the sad problem of "emigrants who seek work"; this may happen at times as a "necessary evil," but still the man who must work outside of his own country must be accorded fully equal rights with those of the native workers. "It is not true," argued John Paul II before the workers at St. Denis, "that the worker has no homeland. In a special way he is the representative of his people; he is a man with his own house; and to him is owed, since he is away from home, double solicitude and understanding" (to workers, May 31, 1980).

The pope attributes an absolutely fundamental significance to farm work. "The right to land does not cease to be the foundation of a sound economy and sociology" (homily at Nowy Targ, June 8, 1987). This is why the social situation of the workers and their just rights must be taken into consideration, not to say re-evaluated in the scale of the entire economy. And his words do not refer only to the situation of Polish agricultural workers. "Many deformations of rural life find their cause in the inferior condition of the farmer as a worker and as a citizen. For this motive also, the image of the farmer, or of the so-called farm laborer, who works excessively and with scant results, should be replaced by the image of an efficient and independent producer, aware of, capable of using (no less than others) the benefits of culture, and who can increase it" (homily during Mass of Beatification of K. Kozka, Tarnow, June 10, 1987). From the entire pontifical teaching there emerges the conviction that agricultural work is a special image of God, and that it is the key to understanding his kingdom (*ibid.*).

On the basis of the rights previously enumerated, there rests clearly the further right to group together in defending the interests of the working class, and therefore, before all others, the right to form syndicates which are, obviously, "independent and free" (homily to workers, Gdansk-Zaspa, June 12, 1987). Contrary to the Marxist view, John Paul II does not consider their existence simply as a manifestation of structure, "of classes" in society, nor does he think that they constitute a claim for uncontrolled "class struggle." "They are, in deed, a mouthpiece for the struggle for social justice, for the just rights of working people. . . . However, this struggle should be seen as a normal endeavor 'for' the just good; in the present case, for the good which corresponds with the needs and merits of working people . . . not a struggle 'against others' " (*Laborem Exercens*, 20). Syndicates remain "a constructive factor of social order and solidarity, and it is impossible to ignore it," even when it enters "the field of politics, understood as prudent concern for the common good" (*ibid.*). True, "Union demands cannot be turned into a kind of group or class egoism. However, the role of unions is not to play politics, nor to have the character of political parties struggling for power. They should not be subject to the decision of political parties, or have too close links with them, lest they become an instrument used for other purposes" (*ibid.*).

The same can be said of strikes. They constitute a legitimate instrument of protest, even if it is the "final one" which it is not right to abuse, in particular for the purpose of exerting political pressure. "There can even be a founded opposition by unionists"; but this, however, should not represent "political forces extraneous to the workers" (to workers, Buenos Aires, April 10, 1987, and Quito, January 30, 1985).

"And thus," the pope warns, "structures in themselves do not guarantee either justice or cooperation" (to workers, Bottrop, May 2, 1987). So that these results may be obtained substantially it is indispensable that the spirit of solidarity should animate them. In the doctrine of John Paul II we find still another key phrase: "Solidarity is a basic word in the history of the working class, and today it is a gospel word" (to workers at Laeken, May 19, 1985). These expressions belong to the unceasing message of the Church's social teaching. The idea of the solidarity of the world of work penetrates, while surpassing them, "systems, structures, ideologies. . . creating a specific 'civilization of solidarity' " (to ILO, Geneva, June 15, 1982). In fact, "what does *Solidarnosc* mean?" asked the Holy Father of Polish sailors, the Polish workers who created in a forthright yet peaceful way, in August, 1980, the union called "Solidarnosc." "Solidarnosc means one manner of being in unity, amid human multiplicity; for instance, of the nation, with respect for all the differences and diversities which exist among men. Hence, unity in diversity, pluralism. . . a manner of being amid human diversity, greater or less, of all humanity, of every nation, of existence in a unity worthy of man. Solidarity is something to be conquered, I add that solidarity inspires struggle. . . a struggle for man. . . when

it allows itself to be guided by truth, liberty, justice, and love"
(to fishermen at Gdynia, June 11, 1987).

Here we have the explanations, the most profound and penetrating explanations, of this fundamental concept in the social teaching of John Paul II. This is an idea which in its essence goes beyond the immediate concern for political agreements, even if it does not refuse them.

VI. TOWARDS A CIVILIZATION OF LOVE
THROUGH WORK AND PRAYER

The Church's duty is not only to pronounce herself on the problems of labor from the point of view of its human value and in reference to the social moral order, but also to elaborate, at the same time, a "spirituality of work in the Christian sense of the term" (*Laborem Exercens*, 24). The elements of this spirituality of work are based on three pillars rooted in the gospel. Not by chance did the Holy Father entitle the last three chapters of the encyclical *Laborem Exercens,* "Work as a sharing in the activity of the Creator; Christ, the Man of work; and Human work in the light of the Cross and of the Resurrection of Christ."

It is important, finally, to dwell briefly on the manner in which Christian spirituality in the experiences of life permeates the sphere of work and its material; for, as the pope teaches, "without the contrary action which is inspired by spiritual principles and values, work becomes a senseless grind, the aspiration towards progress is blind; the race for more production loses all sense of measure" (to workers, Bottrop, May 2, 1987). Prayer is the element which unites, which binds. The bond between prayer and work has an organic character. The motto of the Benedictine monks, *ora et labora*, laid the foundations of the great Christian edifice of Europe. John Paul II presented this bond in the fullest manner during his pilgrimage to Poland, in his homily to the faithful of Upper Silesia and of Zagla Dabrowski, the two industrialized regions of Poland. "And this is why I once again turn my eyes. . . towards the blast furnaces and the smokestacks of the factories; it is a land of much work and of much prayer. Both are tightly bound together in the traditions of this people, whose most common greeting is 'God help you!' words which join the thought of God with human work, and make reference to it" (homily to the faithful, Czestochowa, June 6, 1979).

Immediately afterwards, in that same talk, the pope thanked God because here, the progress of human labor has gone ahead "at the same pace with the building of churches, with the opening of parishes, with the deepening and the reinforcement of the faith. Progress has not involved dechristianization, the breaking of that alliance which in the human soul should be found joining labor and prayer according to the motto of the Benedictines: *ora et labora*. In all human work prayer brings in a reference to God, Creator and Redeemer, and contributes at the same time to the total humanization of labor. Do not let yourselves be seduced by the temptation that man can truly find himself by turning his back on God, by cancelling prayer from his life, and remaining nothing but a worker, deceiving himself that what he produces alone can fill the needs of the human heart. 'Not from bread alone does man live' " (*ibid.*).

The natural link between work and prayer is expressed in the fullest manner at the culminating and most important moment of the Mass. "The Eucharist is organically linked with human labor, as the words of the offertory affirm. We bring to the altar the bread; but this bread, fruit of the earth, is at the same time the work of human hands. . . . We pray that this may become for us 'food of eternal life.' These words refer to the body of Christ. He in fact is for us the 'food of everlasting life' in the sacrament of his body and blood, the Eucharist. Human work is for material ends. Man works for his daily bread. Christ, the Savior of the world, has made this bread, at the same time, a visible sign, that is, the sacrament of eternal life" (to workers at Uniontex, Lodz, June 13, 1987).

When on the beach at Dantzig John Paul II thanked the workers of the coastal navy yards who in 1980 had taken upon themselves hard work upon hard work, he stressed also that this task had been taken up "before Christ and his Mother" (homily during Mass at Gdansk, June 12, 1987). By this very act he gave to those events a clear religious symbolism, and aroused the admiration of the entire world. In that same year, 1980, at St. Denis, the pope had asked the French workers: "By what right have this moral force, this willingness to struggle for the truth, this hunger and thirst for justice, been systematically, and even in public pronouncements, separated from the words of our Mother?. . . In the name of what has the struggle for justice in the world been linked with the program of a radical denial of God?" (May 31, 1980).

There clearly appeared that there did not exist any right, or any claim of such a kind. The Polish working class had demanded their rights, with the gospel in hand. "Work and Christ? Work and the Eucharist? This is what happened here. And rightly. . . In every holy Mass, in the sacrifice of Christ, the sacrifice of our salvation, there enters the fruit 'of human hands' of all human work. The bread is the synthetic expression of it, and so is the wine. Daily, human work enters into the Eucharist, into the sacrament of our salvation. Great mystery of faith! Every day, in so many places on the earth, before human work divine perspectives open up" (homily to workers, Gdansk, June 12, 1987).

Peace and order among men are based on justice. Only prayer makes human work find a place in that order which is truly such according to the Christian measure: the order of love. The vision of John Paul II appears as an integral one: "A true culture of work is a culture of justice, and leads at the same time to a civilization of love" (homily to workers, Concepcion, April 5, 1987).

To be precise, it must become that stable civilization of love in which pre-eminence is given to ethics over technology, to the person over things; the superiority of the spirit over matter (cf. *Redemptor Hominis*, 16; homily at Bird's Hill Park, Winnipeg, September 16, 1984).

Prayer and man's work will bring us towards such a civilization of love. Human labor, saturated with prayer.

Jozef Cardinal Glemp
Archbishop of Warsaw
(Poland)

(Translated by Richard Arnandez, FSC)

FAITH AND CULTURE IN THE
TEACHING OF JOHN PAUL II

Bishop Alessandro Maggiolini

In striking continuity with Paul VI, John Paul II in his teaching considers the topic of culture as one of the most significant elements in his own pastoral and evangelizing activity.

This is due especially to the fact that Pope Wojtyla centers his teaching on "the person of Christ," that is, the human being, not in his ideal generic character and his abstract essence, but in his historical situation, as a being created by God and destined to find his completeness — whether he knows this or not — in the Lord Jesus.

It seems obvious that in this perspective it will be most interesting to discern, above all, the relationship that the Roman Pontiff discovers in revelation between faith and culture, or, in other words, between Christian and human values.

Before beginning, however, we must clarify certain notions found in the pope's teaching.

I. THE CONCEPT OF CULTURE

1. Ambiguities to be overcome

John Paul II does not limit himself to the concept of culture as the generic refinement of the mind, and, as a consequence of this refinement, products such as works of thought, art, science, and so on. Nor does he identify culture with information or erudition. Still less does he join the school of thought that indiscriminately opposes "culture" to "nature." Culture, flowing from the consciousness and the initiative of the human person delivers the person from the limits — the slavery — of nature seen as something totally manipulatable. Still less does he adopt the point of view of a certain "structuralism," according to which the person as a responsible subject does not exist; culture would be a system of convictions and customs which would exist in so far as they arise from a collectivity coordinated in time and/or space.

We can see clearly the motives for rising beyond these — and other similar — concepts of culture. As has been said, the pope poses the person in his actual situation as the determining element of culture.

2. The human person, the subject and term of culture

a) The human being must be considered in his basic reality, as a thinking and free subject, joined with matter indeed, but transcending matter by his spiritual dimension.

Any "reduction" of the person, therefore, shows an inability to grasp him as the maker and at the same time the result of authentic culture. The materialistic "reduction" would end for instance by bringing down the person to the level of being the author of scientific knowledge, of innumerable technical manipulations of the cosmos, and of his own body, or to being the end result of economic relationships. The "spiritualistic" reduction — less frequent, at least in the European and Atlantic traditions — would end by imagining the human being as a being divorced from history, untouched by the earthly problems that surround him: hunger, illiteracy, violence, social injustice.

In addition, the human being must not be looked upon merely as an "individual." He is essentially a social being. He must, then, be considered in his interpersonal relationships: in the family, in intermediate associations based on definite values, in the nation, and in the human race as a whole.

b) If we accept these preliminary principles, we can say that the human being, in the visible world, is the only actual subject of culture, and that he is, at the same time, its sole object and its end. Culture, in fact, is that by which the person *is* more fully, attains a fuller measure of his being. In other words, culture is the person himself who expresses himself, thinks and acts, who creates certain determined contexts of values and of behavior, and by these is helped or hindered in his efforts to become fully what he should be.

Obviously, it is not possible to identify culture with nature. Yet nature, in so far as it is the actual basic datum, cannot be forgotten, still less denied. Nature has, written into itself, the moral laws governing the person's action according to truth, goodness, and beauty. This is why, while holding to the unchanging essence of the human being, we can still emphasize diverse features of certain aspects of his person, without neglecting other aspects, which are also determining. In other words, there can be varying valid cultures. This is also why by his free choice the person can manifest himself in cultures which are less authentic, or even aberrant, when these contradict the normative ethical exigencies which he bears within himself.

c) In another way one can describe culture not so much as a collection of disparate notions, but as norms of value-judgments and actions performed which are proper to the person. These norms governing value-judgments and actions permeate and codify the social structures on which the person depends, and which the person himself can provoke or modify.

II. THE CONCEPT OF FAITH

1. Contrasts and limitations

For what concerns faith too, it may be useful to clarify certain points.

a) To believe is not a merely emotive act, characterized by all the fragility and the inconstancy of feelings.

Nor is it a voluntaristic act which the person would elicit for no "reasons" at all, or still less, in opposition to reason. To be a human thing, faith must be prepared for and supported by "proofs" of the intellectual, philosophical, and historical orders, even if these "proofs" do not, in strict logic, lead to necessary conclusions; for the decision to believe is at once the result of an intervention by God who manifests himself, illuminating and stimulating the person, and of a free response elicited by the person himself who yields himself fully to God who calls him.

b) From the cognoscitive point of view faith, therefore, means holding as true certain statements concerning God, humanity, and created reality, based not on objective evidence or demonstrations, but on the authority of God who is absolute Truth, and who, as such, can neither deceive nor be deceived.

In this sense, to believe means, in some measure and some manner, to perceive reality with the "mind" of Christ himself.

We should not forget that human intelligence not only prepares the way for faith, but also fulfills a role of its own within the act of faith itself: it seeks to understand, as far as is humanly possible, the mystery of God; and at the same time it respects the mystery in its "super-rational" dimension, which has nothing in common with the absurd.

2. The "new creature" and the people

a) When faith achieves its fullness in conversion, then not only are the intelligence and the will moved by grace and made capable of penetrating into the divine universe revealed by God; it is the person himself in his wholeness who is changed from the super-natural point of view, and made a sharer in the life of Christ. Then the person can think, having as his criteria of truth and value the criteria of Christ the Lord himself; he hopes and loves dependently on, and directed by, the Lord Jesus; he acts by following and participating in the realistic "model" of the Lord Jesus, thanks to the gifts of the Spirit.

And all this takes place without any diminution in the fundamental reality of the person, in his being and action; rather, this reality is promoted (in a certain sense it is autonomous) to the perfection of sharing in divine life.

b) Faith is not an act, or an attitude, or a transformation of the person, taken in isolation and separated from all and from everything else. The believer becomes fully such because he is an element in and a member of a people which is the Church.

We speak not only of the Catholic believer, conscious of his faith, but also of those who live, in good conscience, in non-Catholic Christian communities, or in the world's great religions, or even in the human race itself, which is as a whole called to salvation in the name of Christ. All these, in different ways and at various levels, are called to faith — at least an implicit faith — and normally they experience this faith in social structures.

This statement does not mean to describe the various religious groups in a relativistic sense, as though all of them were equally true and equally efficacious. Rather, it aims, evidently, at drawing attention to the fact that there is certain symbiosis between the cultural and the religious dimensions of the person's life. While recognizing that the various human and religious structures found in the world are not free of limits and errors, a consequence of sin in the human being, these structures aim at finding in the Church a true and full capacity for being instruments of grace and truth. Analogically, one might say as much for the non-Catholic Christian communities which, however, do objectively possess certain redemptive means which are derived from Christ.

III. AN ORGANIC RELATIONSHIP

1. Various hypotheses

In the light of the notions we have been trying to elucidate, various hypotheses can be offered, or, if one prefers, we can note various conceptions and practices referring to the relationship between faith and culture. We can reserve the right to make a calm criticism of those aspects in which they do not correspond with the "logic of the Incarnation" which John Paul II stresses.

a) We can, and must, point out a possible or existing contrast between faith which, on the one hand, safeguards and protects humanity in the person, especially his intelligence; and certain determinate cultures on the other.

This eventuality, or this *de facto* situation finds its motivation, as we remarked above, not only in the structural limitedness of the human being, but in the historical recognition of the sin that the human being commits, and by which he is, as it were, dominated.

In this view we must admit, not that the person is extraneous to culture, but that he draws his origin and is conditioned by a culture which does not correspond either with the person's requirements, or, even less, with the requirements of Revelation and faith.

Let this be admitted without negating the germs of truth and of grace which even the most corrupt culture may offer, as a fruit of research and ethical efforts; and especially as a fruit of the action of the Holy Spirit in various historical or geographical contexts.

b) Another possible hypothesis — which has at times been reduced to theory, and practiced — is the one which sees faith and culture as two realities merely juxtaposed to each other. At most there could be between faith and culture some sporadic, occasional opposition, which, however, would not have any influence on either of the two components, save in extrinsic terms.

Here we must affirm the principle that on the intelligible plan reason and faith can never be in contradiction to each other, given that both have God as their sole source, and both refer to reality which is created by God and which cannot contradict itself. Still, we must recognize the narrowness of this point of view. Faith is not merely knowledge, but a total re-making of the person in Christ. Reason, while autonomous in a certain sense, and up to a certain point, is not extraneous to faith, but prepares the way for faith and waxes more vigorous within faith.

This hypothesis, moreover, would be not only narrow in range, but simply erroneous if it sought to separate faith and culture, as though culture were a self-sufficient sphere, unaffected by the influence of Revelation and of God's gift of himself in Christ; as though the person were imagined to be individualized and interiorly dissociated.

In reality, in the light of God's word, there is no such thing as "pure nature" or an "uncorrupted person" to which the "supernatural" would be "superadded" in an extrinsic, not to say disturbing manner. There exists a nature wounded as a consequence of original sin, of the "sin of the world," and of personal sin; but this nature is at the same time called to share in the knowledge and the life of Christ. There exists a person, corroded by evil, but invited to surpass himself through grace — through grace which is accepted by individuals, but normally within the salvific context of the Church or of other forms of religion related to the Church as to their own fullest expression.

c) A third hypothesis which might be — and sometimes is — advanced, is that of a relationship of reciprocal absorption between faith and culture. Either it is affirmed that culture is destined to disappear in faith; or, more frequently, it is maintained that faith must lose its own originality and be dissolved in culture.

In the first case, that is, that culture must be absorbed by faith, we would have a sort of "integrism" which wants to sacralize everything, which pretends to do away with the consistency of the person's creaturehood and with his expressions of it; which seeks to exhaust the mystery of Christ within the bounds of a historical form of human society, one that is, therefore, limited and transitory.

In the second case, that is, that faith must dissolve in culture, we would have a total misunderstanding of the originality of

Christianity, a theory in which culture would end up by being the motive of our salvation, and not the Lord Jesus accepted into people's minds and lives.

In either case the unique character of the human person would be overshadowed; the person would cease to appear as a responsible being, created and redeemed — or at least called to Redemption — and his social component would be denied.

2. The "logic of the Incarnation"

a) John Paul II, on the contrary, speaks of an "organic and constitutive" link, a "fundamental link" which must be established between faith and culture. He affirms that faith must "illustrate," "purify," "renew," "pervade," "inform," "saturate," "create," "become" Christian culture or the Christian cultures, if we keep in mind the variety of contexts.

This means that we need to rise beyond all contrasts and all dualism. Christian newness must be able not only to refute error and non-values, and welcome, purify and bring to completion the germs of truth and of grace which it meets; it must also be able to create untried social organizations, inspired by the principles of the gospel. All this without annihilating the relative autonomy of the creature-components, without expecting to capture in one, or even several, cultures the inexhaustible riches of the mystery revealed by God; without compromising the liberty of each and every person.

b) To sum up: we might review the reasons why faith should generate a Christian culture.

We find the first in the historical order. Nor should this reason be considered *a priori* of little worth, if we notice the constant character of this phenomenon. In fact, Christianity throughout its entire existence has come into contact with various cultural systems, and has renewed them through its evangelical principles. Moreover, it has sometimes even brought into being new cultural systems, thanks to the formative influence of its presence and its proclamation.

A second reason belongs to the sociological or pastoral order. It consists in the fact that the human person cannot be abandoned in a situation of unbearable dissociation where, on the one hand, he must think and live in Christian terms, and on the other, he is constrained to function in a zone of understanding and behavior estranged from, if not hostile to, his faith. Paul VI called this dichotomy one of the most disastrous elements of our times, as regards evangelization. And John Paul II re-using the same formula and pursuing the same line of thought as his predecessor, insists on underlining the obligation we have of Christianizing our culture so that to all may be given the possibility of living their faith without encountering useless or harmful hindrances. To give up the effort to create a Christian culture means — whether we intend this or not — to exclude the "poor" from the proclamation of the gospel, and to reserve the explicit experience of faith to the few persons possessing remarkably keen judgment and unusual courage. (But why, then, do these few persons not attempt to help their less gifted brethren by communicating to them what they need most, and striving to prepare for them a milieu that might protect and stimulate their Christian life?)

However, the deepest reason for the constitutive link between faith and culture lies in the theological order.

If belief is not "something" that is added to a person; if it is not a partial and sporadic gesture, but a modification of the person himself in his total being — in his manner of thinking, in his evaluative criteria, in his manner of acting — then it is hard to see why faith should not lead people to take on the responsibility for creating a Christian culture.

This affirmation — if misunderstood — may be at the origin of an unacceptable intolerance which betrays itself in an improper "ecclesiasticalization" of civil society, and which lies at the source of a failure to recognize the creature-side of the person's makeup. But these dangers will be avoided if the basic rights of all are respected — including the right to religious liberty, and especially if due account is taken of the unity of the plan of salvation which recovers, corrects and perfects the creation spoiled by sin in the world, and in the person himself.

IV. THREE APPLICATIONS

To conclude, it may be opportune to suggest at least three duties — among many others — regarding the application of what we have been stating here.

1) Evangelization

Clearly, one of the first duties flowing from faith is that of evangelization. This, in the name of Christ's command, in the name of the very dynamics of faith itself. It seeks to take away ignorance and error from the "world," in the sense that John and Paul understood the term; it seeks to deliver from sin, which can occur even outside of the Church (need we point this out?); it seeks to bring together in the Church, as the Acts of the Apostles express it, those who are converted and who precisely in the Church bring to completion the evangelical expectations that the Spirit has stirred up in them. . . . In the Church which, objectively speaking, possesses as a gift not only the fullness of truth and grace in Christ, but also the instrumentallies for knowing ever more deeply and for assimilating ever more thoroughly the truth and grace in Christ.

It goes without saying that the evangelical approach can and must be addressed to individuals; but it should also address itself to the cultures in which individuals find themselves involved.

Again it goes without saying that there does not exist a Christianity "in the pure state" which is to be communicated. Instead, there exists a Christianism already "incarnated" in a certain culture, to be transmitted to other cultures willing to welcome it.

2) Dialogue

Thus dialogue appears as a means of evangelization, not as an end in itself.

Dialogue means approaching another, listening to the reasons he may have, and accepting the valid points contained in what he has to say. But dialogue also means courage in presenting oneself under one's genuine aspect, and in offering the most decisive arguments for what one thinks, and the most basic motives for the way one lives. One must intend to initiate a search which does not stop at oneself, in a morbid cultivation of doubt, but which seeks to find truth.

Carried on with faith, this dialogue will not be addressed to two interlocutors, but to three: the believer, the one who does not yet believe—or the "unconscious Christian"—and the Master, who is the Spirit of the Lord Jesus. In this sense the Christian will offer and seek to justify his own convictions and his personal experience of grace. But he will not neglect to receive with gratitude the germs of truth and life that the same Spirit may have sown in the "other." Indeed, these germs will incite the believer himself to make explicit, and to test out, the unplumbed riches of the mystery which he already possesses in Christ, but which he still has not fully exploited, not yet applied totally to the concrete details of his existence.

Paradoxically, dialogue when genuine produces an enrichment of the faith.

And we must insist on underlining that dialogue need not be carried on only in an interpersonal context; it should also be attempted in intercultural situations. One must even foresee clashes when dealing with cultural milieux that are especially poor, rigid, and closed till they reach the level of ideologies.

3) Christian society

If faith does not stop at discussion but tends towards action, the attempt to inaugurate evangelization and dialogue is bound to animate societies in an evangelical manner, in their public expressions of customs, laws, rites, etc.

In this connection the pope does not make use of the term "Christianity," perhaps because of the ambiguities which this might give rise to. But this does not mean that, in principle, we either idealize or condemn Christian history. If by Christianity we understand the responsibility for creating a civil mode of living permeated with evangelical values, in the total respect of liberty for all, then it is not easy to understand why faith would fail to develop in the direction of "Christianities," diversely actuated in different states — especially under democratic regimes — precisely through a culture originally inspired by Revelation and faith.

These will be partial "Christianities," minority groups, careful not to pre-empt all the elbow-room needed for social living. But in the last analysis, there does not exist one "model" Christianity. What do exist are attempts at humanizing society within the limits of what is possible and opportune, by bringing the evangelical spirit into public structures, without forcing anyone into the faith, and by creating free associations more explicitly correlated with the faith. The Church herself should have her own role, as an established community, which is also sociologically significant.

If we think it over carefully we do not succeed in understanding how, even among Catholics, we theorize about the end of Christianity and about how impossible it is to propose it, without splitting hairs. Unless, behind this attitude there hides an individualistic and ritualistic faith which is not supposed to show itself, or to influence history. Whereas, on the contrary the faith which develops into a culture can be a powerful and indispensable help which safeguards and stimulates the ethical values capable of sustaining and renewing the unity of peoples who wish to protect and to promote the person in his integrity.

In this perspective, the promotion of the human being which is a constitutive dimension in evangelization, disentangles itself from an individualistic bind, and even becomes a public activity in the upbuilding of a free and equal city. All this without denying the gratuitous character of love, but still without making it a mere instrument — raising it, rather, to be the guardian of justice.

Bishop Alessandro Maggiolini
Bishop of Como (Italy)

(Translated from Italian by Richard Arnandez, FSC)

THE SIGNIFICANCE OF THE APOSTOLIC LETTER OF JOHN PAUL II TO THE YOUNG PEOPLE OF THE WORLD

Bishop Paul Cordes

On March 31, 1985 John Paul II addressed an apostolic letter to the youth of the entire world. This Letter offers not only a summary of the pedagogical-catechetical orientation that the pope wishes to give to the youth of today. Upon examining it we see that it reflects the typical way in which the Holy Father communicates the gospel to the youth of the world in our time. The Letter constitutes something absolutely new in the history of the Church; never before had a pope addressed to young people a letter as personal and as detailed as this one; never before had a pope dialogued so directly with the young, reflecting on the basic questions that confront them.

Why did John Paul II do this? What impelled him to take this step?

Mere speculation on the reasons which inspired this Letter of the Holy Father to the young people of the entire world cannot lead to certain answers. But it can point to certain indications which take away from the Letter much of its extraordinary character, and show it to be highly logical, not to say strictly necessary.

POSSIBLE MOTIVES, AND OBJECTIVES SOUGHT

What might be called the "external" reason for the message was the International Year of Youth sponsored by the United Nations Organization. Indeed, right at the beginning of the Letter the pope refers to this "Year" which takes on a special significance for the Church also, since "she is the guardian of fundamental truths and values" (chapter 1). It is particularly during youth, says the Holy Father, that every person must forge the key that will permit him to discover and appropriate to himself both truth and values. The Letter, then, is based on the conviction that, in the dialogue with the young and about the young the Church cannot remain mute. Indeed, in our day, the Church has important attitudes and experiences which she must pass on for the greater good of the young themselves.

A glance over the contents of every one of the pope's doctrinal documents shows that this most recent publication follows in logical sequence. Besides his encyclicals which develop theological truths, like *Redemptor Hominis*, or *Dives in Misericordia*, John Paul II has often taken up positions in the fields of specialized pastoral concerns. There are, for instance, his annual Holy Thursday letters to priests, in which, for instance, he reflects among other things on the priest's self-understanding; there are apostolic documents like *Familiaris Consortio* on the family, and *Salvifici Doloris* on human suffering. And when he showed for the first time to some of his helpers the idea of a letter to young people, the Holy Father indicated that he wanted to give a certain systematic thrust to his teaching.

He was, moreover, impelled by his natural affection for youth. When he called them "the hope of the Church" this was not just to win their sympathy or attract their attention. The interest the pope shows in young people is obvious whenever he is with them, be it in the courtyard of San Damaso in the Apostolic Palace, on a summer evening, or in the course of an audience granted to some young organization in Paul VI hall, or during a visit to the International Youth Center of San Lorenzo in Rome. Anyone who has never attended such meetings should be convinced if he looks at the statistics. In 1985 the Pontifical Council for Laypersons published a volume entitled *The Pope Speaks to Young People* (Vatican Library, 1985). The research made in preparation for this publication brought out certain significant figures. From the beginning of his pontificate until that date the Holy Father had already addressed some 350 discourses to young people — this without counting the general audiences, the visits made to parish churches in Rome, or the talks at the Sunday Angelus. . . occasions when the pope had spoken *to* the young people as well as to others; and without counting the addresses he gave *about* young people, or the documents referring to pastoral work among youth.

Over 350 talks! This figure tells us that for the pope, addressing himself to young people is not a ritual gesture to make a point. There has not been a single pastoral visit in Italy or elsewhere during which the Holy Father did not attempt to have a meeting with young people.

And the response of the young people speaks for itself. In April, 1984, there were 300,000 of them in St. Peter's square. "Not even the oldest dwellers in Rome can recall anything like it" commented the ninety-one year old Cardinal Confalonieri, who observed the scene from the terrace of his apartment. The same response came in other circumstances: 300,000 at Lisbon, Portugal; 300,000 at Madrid, Spain; 250,000 in Rome on Palm Sunday, 1985.

Whoever imagines that a pope cannot succeed in "feeling the pulse of our times" or in adopting pastoral initiatives, had better think again. The Holy Father has instituted World Youth Day. He has dealt in his own way with the consequences of what he experienced in the warm welcome given him by the young. By establishing this World Youth Day he clearly wished to encourage the bishops to follow his own example, and meet with the young people of their particular churches on Palm Sunday or on other appropriate days. He himself has twice invited the youth of the world to meet with him in Rome. In the address given at Easter, 1985, he said:

> Last Sunday I met with hundreds of thousands of young people, and I still bear, engraved on my soul, the joyful image of their enthusiasm. While hoping that this marvelous experience may be repeated in future years, giving a start to World Youth Day on Palm Sunday, I repeat my firm conviction: youth is facing a difficult but exciting task — that of transforming the fundamental "mechanisms" that, in relationships between individuals and nations promote selfishness and abuse of others; and that of bringing into being new structures inspired by truth, solidarity, and peace. But may the young remember that to succeed in changing structures, they must first of all change hearts. Peace is born in the person's heart; and it dies there too. (*Insegnamenti*, III/2, 936)

On precise orders from the pope a special theme is chosen every year for World Youth Day. This year, specially dedicated to the Mother of God, the watchword is Mary's own: "Do whatever he tells you." This day shows that the truths of faith influence us in various ways; of course they apply first of all to our interior life; but they do not remain shut up therein. This is important also because it strengthens the bond between young people, the gospel, and the teaching of the Church. It also makes them experience their own togetherness: the first celebration of this day on a worldwide scale gathered around the pope in Buenos Aires about a million young people.

The need for a Master and Model

Clearly, the pope knows how to touch the young. He strikes the right note. Nor is this all. Obviously, a great many young people recognize him as a man who can teach them how to face up to life, how to approach faith in a new way. Why then should the Holy Father feel obliged to give up the idea of proclaiming Christ to the young in a more lengthy written document? Why, since they pay so much attention to him? As a philosopher he has given much thought to the "sequela" and — as he himself says — to the ethical dynamism of the human person. Following in the footsteps of Max Scheler, he affirms that the personal ethical values an exemplary man displays provoke the immediate formation of analogous values in his disciples. "Only the action of universal moral norms threatens the autonomy of the ethical conscience and of the will in the one who is receiving such norms. On the contrary, when the ideal is seen embodied in a model, the autonomy of the conscience and will on the part of the disciple who imitates remains intact. In fact, the complete influence of the model is based on the love felt for the person of the Master-Model, and it is precisely this love which is a substantial source of the cognoscitive sense of values which should constitute the object of the will" (*I fondamenti dell'ordine etnico* [Bologna: Ed. Dehoniane, 1980], 170-171). When, in 1957, Karol Wojtyla wrote those lines, he could certainly not have imagined that he himself would live them in his own person amidst so many young people.

Often enough, today, the theories about the "religious hunger" experienced by young people are called into question. But the Holy Father must have received a confirmation of this experience in his own meetings with the young. There are, in fact, other indications besides the number of young people who come in answer to his invitation. Let me give just a few instances. A study on "the condition of youth in Italy" provides information also on "the Catholic world." The results of the survey were compared with those of a similar study made in 1969. We are told: "The feeling that the Church has regained, or is regaining a major role in socialization of the young is indirectly confirmed by two other findings. The first is the position which religious organizations (especially in the parishes) occupy in the hierarchy of youth associations. . . . The second sign of a re-found capacity for cohesion in the Catholic world is given to us by an analysis of the correlation between age and religious associations."

Regarding Germany, we may allude, although in a less precise manner, to the great number of young people who, every other year, take part in the *Katholikentag*. Often they make up two thirds of the participants, and from 1970 to the present the mass media has always called attention to this fact, with unfailing surprise.

Another indication comes to us from a study made by the Latin American Bishops Conference which shows, among other things, that the young are always more attracted to the Church wherever she is credible, and stands with the people. Here we should remember that 74 million Latin Americans—that is, one out of five—are between fifteen and twenty-four years old. In 1980 the young people between the ages of ten and twenty-four made up one third of the working population of Latin America. These figures reveal the extent to which "youth" counts in this area of the world.

The last indication which I would like to offer, as a sign of the growing interest of the young in religious matters, is a change of direction in the number of religious vocations. From 1979 to the present the number of priestly ordinations has been increasing, world-wide, at a slow but constant rate; and in the major seminaries the number of candidates for the priesthood has risen significantly.

All these positive signs should not lead us to believe that the world of the young today is "radiant with hope"! This would not only be untrue, but from the pastoral point of view it would be a fatal mistake. There are, however, signs which indicate that the time is favorable for the Church's mission. This is a conclusion drawn from analyses centered not specifically on young Christians, but on the youth scene in general, and which examine the worst varied elements found in the mentality of today's youth. The German Jesuit, Fr. R. Bleistein, an expert in youth work, in a radio address about young people, declared: "Most young people are concerned with questions and experiences of a religious character. To problems such as liberty or the lack of it, peace, justice, love, the person's uniqueness (what young person wants to be just another number?) they seek answers which are absolute and final. These questions show an opening towards religion, a religious anxiousness in the young. But how can the Church find them? How does she speak to them? How can she lead them on the path towards Jesus?"

In this same radio address Fr. Bleistein expressed no complacency concerning the work done among the young up to now by the responsible persons in the Church. He was very tentative, and even found much to criticize. Among other things, he asked: "Is the Church losing its young people?" And he even added, "Is the Church driving the young away?"

At least as far as he is concerned, the pope certainly does not act thus. His letter to the young and its contents are a further proof of his interest in young people and of his love for them.

TWO PARALLEL NOTES IN THE LETTER

The Holy Father did not intend to write a "manual" for those engaged in youth work. This was simply because the decisive facts on which pastoral action is based result from the circumstances and the concrete situations of life which change from day to day, from one cultural milieu to another, from one political system to another.

Young people are extremely diverse, and to address all of their concerns in the same letter would be an impossible task. The pope, however, poses the typical questions young people ask, and discusses the fundamental decision common to all of them. He does not so much present them with concrete models of individual or collective behavior, but shows rather the values which should determine the behavior of the young person in his own situation. This corresponds precisely with the studies of Karol Wojtyla, the philosopher, on the importance of phenomenology in the transmission of moral attitudes.

If one were to seek for models of this letter in the classical texts on the guidance of people, he would not find them either in political writings or in those concerned with pastoral theology. If one wanted an example, he might take into consideration the *Philothea* of St. Francis de Sales, or the *Letters on Self-Forma-*

tion by Romano Guardini. Here I cannot go into details; but this might suffice. The pope's letter resembles Guardini's work in the realistic, but always benevolent way in which it "measures" the life-concerns of the young. There is no compromise as regards the high demands of ethics, but the author always lets his human touch and his benevolence shine through.

Speaking of experiences such as love, friendship, engagement and matrimony, we read: "Many times in my life I have had the opportunity of following up more closely, in a certain sense, this love among young people. Thanks to this experience I have understood how essential is the problem we are considering here, how important it is, and how great" (chapter 10). Such understanding, and such an ability to share the "other's" concerns, create in the reader the willingness to let himself be guided.

The Letter is also akin to the *Philothea* of St. Francis de Sales because of its constant openness to God and Jesus Christ. This openness is evident in the second chapter, where John Paul II comments on the well-known passage containing the dialogue between Jesus and the rich young man (cf. Mk 10:17-22). He places the reader in contact with the Lord, and makes it possible for him to dialogue with Jesus Christ. I quote: "Allow me, therefore, at most, to join my reflections in this Letter with this encounter, and with this gospel passage. Perhaps in this way it will be easier for you to continue your own conversation with Christ—a conversation which is fundamentally important and essential for any youth" (chapter 2).

Obviously, one of the main purposes of the Letter is precisely the intention of directing the reader towards an existentially effective union with God. After the phrase: "And then Jesus, fixing his eyes on him, loved him," we read: "I wish that each one of you may discover this gaze of Christ and experience it in the depths of your being. I do not know at what moment of your life this may happen; but I think that it will be when your need is greatest, perhaps in a time of suffering, perhaps together with the testimony of a pure conscience, as was the case for this young man in the gospel; or perhaps even in the opposite situation, with a realization of your sinfulness and with remorse of conscience. Christ, indeed, looked upon Peter in the hour of his fall, when he had thrice denied his Master. This loving look is necessary for the person; for he needs to realize that he is loved, loved eternally, and chosen from   all eternity" (chapter 7).

This scene, once sketched, remains the locus for all the reflections that follow. A locus which is not given up even at the end of the Letter. Indeed, the various verses and notions found in this passage are used to introduce and to develop various significant aspects in the unfolding life of young people.

The entire spectrum of questions about life is taken up: the young man's wealth (chapter 3); conscience and commandments, value and truth (chapter 6); Christian and religious vocation (chapter 8-9); the family and the social community as the roots of the individual (chapter 11).

In chapter 12, speaking of schools and formation we read: "At school you must acquire the intellectual, technical, and practical skills which will enable you to take your place usefully in the great workshop of human labor. But if it is true that school should prepare you for work, even manual work, it is also true that work in itself is a school that teaches great and important values."

Work! Today so many young people experience it as looking for work, or lack of work. The pope formulates as follows this agonizing concern of the young: "You ask yourselves, 'Does society need me?' 'Can I too find adequate work which will enable me to make myself independent?' In short, 'is it really true that society expects my contribution?' "

Elsewhere the Holy Father speaks in favor of the beauty of nature and of culture. "Youth must be a growth process. For this purpose it is enormously important to have contact with the visible world, with nature. This relationship enriches us during our youth in a way that is different from the knowledge of the world which we have drawn from books" (chapter 14).

Even the threats that menace humanity are discussed: war, injustice, poverty, hunger, oppression, persecution. These, according to the pope, are at the source of the dramatic accusations hurled at the adult world by the young. He says: "In these conditions, you young people can rightly ask the previous generations: 'How have we come to this? How have we reached a stage of such grievous threats to humanity on this earth? Why do so many die of hunger? Why are there so many millions of refugees huddled at the frontiers? Why so many cases in which the elementary rights of people are trampled upon? Why so many prisons and concentration camps? so much systematic violence and the murder of the innocent? so much mistreatment and torture perpetrated on people? so much suffering inflicted on human bodies and consciences?' " (chapter 15).

THE SIGNIFICANCE OF THE YOUTH'S TESTIMONY

The Letter of John Paul II to youth has as its motto: "Always be ready to satisfy anyone that asks you for a reason for the hope which is in you" (1 P 3:5). Such questions, problems, dark clouds on the horizon of the present and of the future must not lead the young to pessimism, to a mentality which answers: "No, thanks!"

The pope points to a hope stronger than all the sufferings of this world. And the young, precisely, can give testimony to it.

In the first place, therefore, the letter is addressed to the young who are already the bearers of this hope. A hope which, however, is open even to those who seek. His readership is not limited to ecclesiastical circles. The words of the pope are addressed to all young people of good will.

To spread them and make them known is the task of all Christians. Only in this way will this little booklet become, for many young people, even some far from the faith, an important beacon for life.

Bishop Paul Cordes
Vice President, Pontifical
Council for Laypeople

(Translated from Italian by Richard Arnandez, FSC)

5160   6800